SARAH'S STORY

Copyright © 2015 Sarah Barnes

All rights reserved, including the right to reproduction in whole or in part in any form.

ISBN: 978-0-578-15705-4

First Edition, January 2015

Back Cover Design by: Nada Orlic
Interior Book Design by: Mary Jane De Guzman

Every effort has been made to trace copyrights on materials included in this publication. If any copyrighted material has been included without permission and due acknowledgment, proper credit will be inserted in future printings after notice has been received.

Printed in the United States of America on acid free paper.

www.SarahSaysExpressYourself.blogspot.com

TnWriterSarahB@aol.com

The Passions and Perplexities of My Life

Detailed and Recorded in Poems, Essays, and Journals

*Dedicated to my four beloved children,
living proof that in spite of Jer's and my many mistakes
we did manage to do something beautifully right.*

Prologue

— So That's It —
(Summer 1992)

On a mental high, having just returned from my first meeting of a local support group, now I know . . .

Why I make copies of every letter I write. Why they are more like mini-books than letters.

Why I pounded the typewriter every time I felt despondent over Jerry's and my relationship so that by the time the marriage of twenty-two years was over I had amassed five or six dirges of despair. It probably kept me sane.

Why I kept a file called "contemplations" filled with the thoughtful searching that tracked my personal spiritual/ethical evolution from that of a sheltered, trusting, naive, conservative 22-year-old Christian to the skeptical, liberal Christian with Unitarian leanings that I am today. (Which is another way of saying the older I get, the smaller I get, the bigger God gets. What I know compared to the knowledge that is, is like comparing one grain of sand on the beach to the beach! It fills me with awe yet makes me peaceful and accepting of this spectacular thing called life).

Why I write yearly epistles I call Christmas letters to my family and close friends which are really encapsulated versions of This Year in the Life of Sarah.

Why I have this compulsion to express my opinion in the Letters To The Editor section of the newspaper whenever I see something on TV or read an article that evokes a strong emotion – sometimes of agreement, more often not.

Why I've written several poems as an adult – even though I could not do so in school when directed to by my teacher. Each time the words came tumbling out of my head almost faster than I could write them down. When I did – and looked at what was written – somehow I knew it was not prose. It was poetry; undisciplined, raggedy maybe, but poetry nonetheless. I've never felt the creative force with such intensity. The first time it happened, I remember thinking, "so this is what a painter feels when he paints. This is why writers write!"

* * * * *

So I'm not crazy, after all. Curious, compulsive, intent. Consumed with the need to express my point of view . . . a writer.

One more piece of the puzzle that makes me . . . me. (And it only took 30 years to find out).

* * * * *

So I'm a writer. So what. Even though the realization has just hit me with inspiring intensity, except for the insight, nothing's changed. I've been writing all my life. At least now I know why. Can I make it count for something other than my own edification?

There's a story in that multitude of words . . . pages and pages of typed words. A story about children and family. About a floundering marriage and its inevitable demise. A spiritual saga. A story of love: teenage love, the idealized love of a naive young woman, and finally of mature love shared by best friends, based not only on chemistry but on mutual trust and respect.

A story about a very ordinary person. And yet . . .

My life – my hopes, my dreams, my trials, my joys – I suspect they're universal to women of my generation in our society.

So if I can do it right – make it funny and sad, interesting and insightful in all the right places – maybe others will want to read it.

And I will have become an **AUTHOR**.

I will be invited to appear on talk shows . . . Oprah, Sally Jessy Raphael . . . Jennie Jones . . And . . . I will be rich!

And then this need to reach out and touch others with my ideas, with the lining of my very soul, will be satisfied. If I get it all said once and for all in a real live book, maybe I can rest. This compulsion will go away and I can relegate my typewriter to the closet and look forward to becoming a contented crone[1] who putters in the garden, reads stories to her grandchildren, snuggles spoon-fashion in bed with her best friend and lover, and reflects in her rocking chair.

"Not likely," say my new friends at the Writers' Support Group. "Don't you know, we never get it all said? That's why we're writers".

Oh . . .

"And don't count on getting rich, either."

Okay . . .

So . . . do it . . .

"In the beginning, Sarah" . . .

---

[1] From Mists of Avalon, by Miriam Bradley, wherein she divides her female characters' lives into stages; crone being the period from 50-70 when a woman is revered for her wisdom and maturity.

– CHILD OF THE FORTIES –

I awake with a start from a vivid dream. A normal occurrence these days; these days of menopause, that is.

Most of the time the dreams are nightmares and I try hard to forget them – or stop them in process. Fortunately, this one was not.

I was dreaming about a childhood friend, Mary Hoffman, who lived next door to us with her five brothers and sisters. They moved away when I was about ten or eleven.

In my dream, Mary and I were together as adults and I was asking her about her family. The more she talked, the more questions kept occurring to me. Are you married? How many children do you have? Are your parents still living? What are your brothers and sisters doing?

All these questions pouring into my head woke me up. As I lay there relishing the dream for a change, I started remembering many things from my childhood; the neighborhood, the house we lived in, the neighbors, the school.

Of course I had to get it down on paper.

So Says Sarah . . .

On Childhood and Youthful Awakenings . . .

SARAH'S STORY

CHILDHOOD MEMORIES
(Written August 1992)

The boundaries of my childhood community in Detroit, Michigan, in the 1940's consisted of the area a few blocks east of Woodward and bounded by State Fair on the north end and Seven Mile Road on the south. We lived at 456 Fernhill which was in the middle of our block. It dead-ended at its east end in a piece of property which was about two acres long and an acre deep.

Railroad tracks ran the length of this property at the back. I spent many summer afternoons perfecting the craft of walking along the raised metal beams of track without falling off. There was a little pond on the property also, which periodically offered up frogs, toads, and tadpoles for science projects. Eventually a small manufacturing company purchased the land and built its offices there.

Goodbye frogs!

Brown's Creamery

My grandmother, Sadie Barnes Hopps, was the store manager of Brown's Creamery on Seven Mile at Carman, a few blocks away. By the time I was eight, I was allowed to walk the eight blocks from our house to her store to visit her and get a 12-cent double-dip ice cream cone – chocolate, of course. They made the best ice cream in the world! On special occasions I would go there with my folks and grandma would treat us all to Hot Fudge Sundaes!

Brown's Creamery doesn't exist anymore so now the closest thing to the best hot fudge in the world is Sanders. Baskin-Robbins isn't even in the running.

The Crazy Lady

Every neighborhood has its crazy lady; naturally, we had ours. And that's exactly what we called her – The Crazy Lady.

But not to her face. She lived in the last house on our side of the street at the opposite end from the railroad tracks. Her front yard was completely fenced and the only time I ever saw her was when she came out to get her paper or her mail. She always looked kind of grey. Disheveled and unkept. Her hair was tangled and her clothes never seemed to match. Often she wore an old bathrobe.

Stories circulated among the kids about how mean she was and what she would do if she caught you. I never planned to find out so I never went inside her yard. (Even on Devil's Night when we kids would take chalk and mark the porch steps of all the houses with "Kilroy Was Here," ring the doorbell, and run like hell – which was about the extent of our delinquency).

I wish I could visit that dear old soul as she was then and as I am now. I would take her some cookies and a lace handkerchief. Maybe she would fix tea. I would sit and hold her hands and talk to her and find out whose child and wife and mother she was. And I would touch her hair and kiss her cheek when I left.

Elementary School

To this day, every trip to Detroit requires a drive down the streets of my childhood and includes a stop at my grammar school, which is only a block and a half from my childhood home; Grayling Elementary. One of those nostalgic odysseys took place during the summer of 1967 and I was hopeful I would be allowed inside. Summer school was in session but it was lunch time. I met a teacher's aid and she took me to the principal who gave me permission to wander through those memory-filled halls once more. I got the feeling they were touched by my sentimentality and slightly amused that I would want to walk the halls and see the classrooms of a school that had obviously seen better days.

I especially wanted to see the library with its beautiful oak window seats. Seeing it reminded me of our librarian, Mrs. Fortune, and the delightful hour I spent each week in "library class" listening to her read aloud from wonderful books like, "Mr. Doolittle and the Talking Animals," "Horton Hatches The Egg," (one of Dr. Seuss' first books), and "A Tree for Peter," by Kate Seredy. It was here that I fell in love with Lucy Montgomery, author of the "Anne of Green Gables" series. (Kate Seredy was a wonderful children's author and her books were beautifully illustrated. Although her books are no longer in print, I managed to find "A Tree for Peter" and "The Chestry Oak," both of which were read by my children and which I have kept for my grandchildren's reading pleasure.)

That beautiful old school has a special place in my childhood memories. Walking through it that summer day fulfilled a special need.

They tore down my high school about twenty years ago. What was once a school is now a Kroger parking lot. So it means a lot to know that my old grade school is still standing. The wooden floors of the classrooms are worn and sagging now – their beauty only enhanced by the thousands of little feet of delightfully active and inquisitive little children who have walked and played and jumped on them and worn them down. Certainly the worse for wear in terms of physical condition, my little school is still providing a valuable service as an oasis for learning in its community.

*****

Through the years, my old neighborhood has gone through several metamorphoses, which I have observed during my necessary periodic pilgrimages. The first time I returned was in my late teens (around 1957-58). The neighborhood seemed sad and shabby. So on my next visit a few years later, I expected to find it the same or worse. But a wonderful thing had taken place. The neighborhood had undergone a facelift. Several homes had been fixed and painted. The well-cared for yards were abloom with flowers.

It didn't last, of course. My last two visits revealed a neighborhood encased in an atmosphere of sadness and defeat, even eliciting a sense of foreboding. Like a candle that burns brightest just before it goes out, the renewal was a last gasp of pride before it succumbed to the ravages of time. As I reminisce about my childhood, I picture my now grey, gloomy, time-weary neighborhood. Mentally I embrace it. I wave my magic wand and it comes to life again in vibrant color as it was in the days of my childhood – a community of wonderfully caring people – many of whom were immigrants and blue-collar workers – and all of whom shared their hearts, their homes, and their time with their neighbors.

June 2, 2013 Update:

They tore down my grade school last week; Grayling Elementary, 744 W. Adeline Street, backing up to State Fair, Detroit, MI 48203. Smashed it to smithereens. It broke my heart.

For two years previous I wrote letters – to school officials, city/county officials . . . emails to congress people.

To no avail. Of course.

I WILL NEVER FORGIVE THEM.

456 Fernhill, Winter 1945

North Side of Fernhill Street, Summer 1998

In 1945, the Robinsons lived in the little house on the right; mom, dad, and one son. The big 2-story house next to them on the left was directly across from 456 (my house) and the Luscitch family lived there. I played with their grand-daughter when she came to visit.

Grayling Elementary School, Summer 1998

From 456 Fernhill, I walked ½ block to the corner, turned right on Havannah and walked one short block to Adeline. Grayling and its playground took up the entire North side of the street with the playground in the back facing State Fair.

Grayling Demolition, May 2013
All That's Left

SARAH'S STORY

11th/12th Grade
English Composition
(1955-56)

I'll Never Do That Again

Are you among the few misled people that think water always puts out a fire? Nine chances out of ten you aren't – at least if you give it any thought. I'm happy to say that I can't be classed in that category – now. But three years ago – . . .

It was on a Friday night in November. My mother was going out to do her weekly grocery shopping and she asked me to cook some french fries. About a week before this we had gotten an electric stove and had put our old gas range in the basement So this was the first time for me to cook on it with no supervision.

First of all, I put the grease on to get hot. I set the potatoes on top of the pan of grease and went into the living room for about five minutes. On our old gas stove it took between five and ten minutes for the grease to get hot. Not so on an electric stove I've since learned.

Anyway, I walked into the kitchen and the grease was on fire. Actually, it wasn't serious, all I would have had to do was set it off the stove and everything would have been fine. But that would have been too simple for me. So I grabbed the pan and literally flung it into the sink. Then, true to form, I turned on the cold water. I don't think I need to explain what happened.

Luckily, my reflexes were pretty good and I jumped back knocking a plate off the table in the process, which promptly broke into several million pieces.

The fire was out by the time I recovered because the chintz curtain over the sink went up in flames so fast the woodwork was merely scorched. Then I looked around the kitchen – nothing makes a bigger mess than smoky grease covering a kitchen ceiling. Some even managed to travel into the corner of the living room ceiling.

I proceeded to open all the doors and windows in an attempt to air out the house considerably. So when my mother and father drove up a few minutes later, they must have thought I was a fresh-air fiend. Until my mother walked into the kitchen. What kept her from fainting I don't know. I guess she isn't the fainting type. She just stood there and finally managed a weak little, "Oh, no."

After I had finished with the gory details, they decided it would be best to have the kitchen redecorated. And since the decorators would already be here they might as well do the living room as it would soon have to be done anyway.

With the decision of the redecorating I had almost decided that maybe my fire wasn't such a bad idea after all. But then I looked up at the kitchen ceiling again and decided . . .

"I'll never do that again!"

— The Princess Years (1952-1956) —

Not J.A.P. Jewish American Princess, that is. Definitely not J.A.P. We weren't Jewish and we certainly weren't rich. Though my father did work for a carpet/floor/tile company owned by two Jewish brothers as their office manager for 25 years. And my mother was raised in the South. (I remember the night Daddy came home from work and announced he was getting a raise, bringing his salary to $10,000 per year; we were so happy!)

Never did I hear either of them denigrate other races or beliefs. Although I was raised in a conservative Christian home, two things stand out in my mind as tenets taught from my mother's/father's knee: never stop searching for truth and never judge "them". There are no "thems". Only people. Treat them individually. Respond to them individually. Turn the other cheek. Try to put yourself in his/her shoes.

In spite of, or maybe because of, these teachings, I took these messages too literally. Approaching the "big 4-0", I stumbled across the book, "Your Erroneous Zones," by Dr. Wayne Dyer and devoured it. It took that age (maturity) and that book to help me develop a decent sense of my own self worth. I finally osmosized (internalized) the concept "so I'm not perfect . . . Who is?"

But I digress. This is supposed to be the part about me and my teenage lover, Nick.

— Teenage Romance – Fifties Style —
(Written in the Summer of 1992)

It All Began . . .

. . . at church. We were fifteen when we started sitting together during Wednesday night services. My dad would drive him home afterwards. His father had died several years before, his mother came only on Sunday mornings, and they didn't own a car. Taking him home was the Christian thing to do. Of course. Which gave us an opportunity to talk some more and hold hands in the back seat.

I remember my dad chauffeuring us to a movie or two but shortly after we began dating, Nick got his driver's license and occasionally managed to bribe his brother-in-law for the use of his car. Within a year, Nick had managed to save enough money to buy his own set of wheels – a black 1950 Ford sedan. It was "leaded in" and had white skirts. We thought we were really cool as we paraded it around the local teenage haunts. Some years later, he managed to buy a 1952 Ford convertible. A red one! We thought it was beautiful, too.

Both those cars provided us many opportunities for the kind of excitement and fun teenagers are wont to pursue. And pursue them we did. With a passion. Literally.[2]

If you were a teenager in the mid-to-late Fifties you may have had a similar experience. Though probably it didn't last quite so long.

It finally came to an end the summer of 1959 when Nick went off to church camp as a counselor and fell in love with the idea of evangelizing the world for Christ – as well as one of the cute little female counselors he met there.

---

[2] Those cars would be Classics now. Sure hope they aren't rusting in a junk heap somewhere in Middle America.

SARAH'S STORY

Bolstered by their love for each other and their renewed dedication to The Word, they would evangelize the world.

But that's their story to tell.

Shortly after Nick and I began Going Together, my parents were preparing for our yearly trek to visit my relatives in Tennessee. Since Nick's grandparents lived in Paducah, Kentucky, I convinced my folks it would be kindness itself to save him the price of a bus ticket by inviting him to go with us. We dropped him off at his grandparents' home the second day of the trip. He took the bus back to Michigan two weeks later.

We had relatives in Camby, Indiana, and this is where we spent the first night. Although our family trip from Michigan to Tennessee can now be made in 9-10 hours, this was prior to expressway travel. The trip took about sixteen hours then and Camby was half way.

Picture a summer sunset in the country. Two shy young teenagers walking hand in hand around the farm checking out the horse, the chickens, and each other. Darkness follows and we sit on the porch talking endlessly. Finally it is time to end this idyllic tryst.

Just before we headed back into the house, Nick reached for my hand and placed his gold signature ring on my left hand as he asked me to Go Steady. My heart was pounding with anticipation and love. Shyly, we kissed. Our first.

And last. At least for the next two weeks. We made do the best we could, however, by writing daily letters filled with our mundane vacation activities and the anticipation of being together again. Included in one of his letters were the words to this song:

> Forever and ever
> My heart will be true.
> Sweetheart forever
> I'll wait for you.

> We both made a promise
> That we'd never part.
> Let's seal it with a kiss
> Forever my sweetheart.
>
> So let's tell the world
> Of our new love divine
> Forever and ever
> You'll be mine.[3]

Is that romantic, or what? . . . Well, if you're fifteen and In Love For The First Time, it is.

* * * * *

As letters go, neither his nor mine would win any awards for literary achievement or profundity, but his to me still reside in a packet tied together with a pink ribbon nestled in a box with other cherished mementos of times and places long ago and far away.

Eventually we got over being shy with each other physically and mentally, of course. The result was that we alternately loved and fought passionately and fiercely for the next seven years. Physically, we inched our way forward, step by exciting new step. We learned and taught each other about love. And talked and read about it, too. No subject was off limits.

We did all the things that teenagers did and do. Football games with sock hops afterwards. Fancy dances with gowns and tuxes and pictures. Beach parties in the summer. One all-night party at a friend's house after his Senior Prom. Wherein we snacked on pop and chips, danced and necked and snuggled until unwanted and unbidden sleep finally claimed us all – around 5 a.m.

---

[3] Lyrics to the song, "Ill Wait for You," recorded by Frankie Avalon, 1958.

Once accomplished, our independence proven, we all agreed staying up all night wasn't THAT much fun.

Like most communities, we had a special Parking Place. Ours was "The Loop". Nestled in a suburban residential area, it was a secluded parking area atop a hill. Cars with 2-6 kids inside would congregate there to visit and make out. We stopped there often on double-dates before calling it a night. Of course on double-dates you really didn't get into heavy petting, mostly it was kissing and hugging, accompanied by whispers and giggles. For one thing, the local police had a way of sneaking up on you and shining their flashlights in the window when you least expected it. So the really serious stuff was saved for more private times.

I remember our first pizza. Pizza parlors were just coming on the scene back then. We ordered a pepperoni pizza to go from a nearby pizzeria, picked up a quart of milk, which we both loved, and headed for The Loop. Once there, we opened the box and got our first look at this new food. It was pretty dark and we thought the pizza looked kind of yucky. It smelled kind of funny, too. Gingerly we took our first bites. "Okay, I guess," we said. With each bite, it tasted better. By the time we finished, we were hooked on pizza for life.

Once in a rare while a smell – or thought – transports me back in time to that night and just for an instant I can actually taste that pizza once more. Nothing – absolutely nothing – has ever tasted quite that good.

* * * * *

Our dates usually ended at my house where we learned and perfected our craft of making out. Till it became making it. Which took a couple of years, actually.

We were trying to be good, you see.

Because . . .

We were the teenagers of the late Fifties. And Christians besides. Good Christian girls didn't Do It. Neither did good Christian boys. Or if they did, they didn't talk about "It". Except to the person they did "It" with.

Conversations full of guilt and fear, delight and joy. Based on secret and furtive couplings full of guilt and fear, delight and joy.

So for a long time we didn't "Do It". Lots of other things we did. Especially I did. We had this misguided concept of morality – based on a mixture of good intentions and rationalization – wherein we decided it was alright for me to do all these things to him – as long as he didn't really Do It to me.

Does any of this sound familiar?

One Sunday afternoon we were driving to visit his aunt. We were sixteen. I was being my usual snugly, affectionate self. I would kiss his cheek, his neck, and run my fingers along the nape of his neck. It drove him wild! I couldn't believe his reaction. It was a powerful feeling!

I don't remember the first time I unzipped his fly – but I know he was driving at the time. We spent a lot of time in his car and I thought it was neat to arouse him when he was driving. The thing that made me bold and allowed me to do things I was taught nice girls didn't, was the reaction it produced. It was like playing a game. If I do this, what will happen? Oh, look, **that's** what happens. It was emotionally thrilling for me, too.

Initially, I learned to make him climax by using my hand. I don't remember when I started using my mouth. I do know it didn't take much convincing on his part. I loved it instantly.

* * * * *

I've never understood women who view the male anatomy with distaste or revulsion. It has always been a thing of beauty and wonder to me. I love it. I wish I had one. But since I don't, I've

SARAH'S STORY

tried to make do with the one closest to me. I believe it's called penis envy.

Don't misunderstand. I love being a woman. The older I get the more admiration and respect I have for the kinder, gentler gender. I do harbor a sneaky suspicion that God probably IS a man, however; SHE would have made our pleasure centers more accessible.

*****

Speaking of penises, however, the night I lost my virginity was at the conclusion of Nick's Senior Prom and took place on my parents' living room floor. We were seventeen. A long way physically and emotionally from that shy night in Camby, Indiana. By now, I had perfected my technique of ministering to that delightful male appendage that responded so fervently to my slightest touch. Nick – and every lover since – claimed I was The Best! (How would He know???). Heady stuff for a teenage girl. Doesn't hurt an old crone's ego, either.

Regarding the events of that night, I don't remember much pain or evidence to mark the occasion. Just lots of excitement. Guilt came later. Even though my parents' bedroom was upstairs, I still marvel at the risk we took. And continued to take over the next four years. And never got caught.

I do remember a few direct questions from my mom from time to time. Like, "What are your panties doing thrown way back in your closet? And what's that stain on them?"

Can you believe I came up with some cockamamie explanation – that she bought? Or at least pretended to. Which only goes to prove there's just some things parents don't want to know.

Not all our couplings took place on the living room floor, of course. In addition to the car, we soon graduated to a studio couch in the den – and the cover on that couch attests to our furtive guilty couplings to this day.

I've often wondered how different this story would have been if Nick had not taken that fateful camp counselor job in the summer of 1959. Because he was the one to make the final break. I was concerned about our frequent and predictable fights. But security was very important to me and I felt safe with Nick. I knew he would never really take advantage of me.

Whenever we broke up, usually every four-five months, we each spent our time pursuing members of the opposite sex. What Nick's track record for those excursions is, I don't know. For myself, although I engaged in some hot and heavy petting sessions, my lack of knowledge and trust in the boy I was with kept me from breaking that self-imposed cockeyed morality that said, "I can do whatever I want to you but We can't Do It.

Maybe it wasn't so cockeyed after all. It prevented pregnancy. And pregnancy, not disease, was the thing we all feared back then. (When I think of some of the crazy bargains I tried to make with God . . .)

Nick and I always had this unspoken understanding that "someday" we would marry. But here we were, 21 years old, going to college, and working part-time. Old enough to marry. Except we never did set a date. He never did actually say, "Sarah, let's do it, let's get married." Getting married was always sometime in the future. For now, we didn't have the money. We needed to finish school. It was never the right time.

If he had actually proposed to me, doubts notwithstanding, I probably would have said yes. (Seven years with him and twenty-two years with my first husband says something about my sense of loyalty, I guess. Which isn't always an admirable trait. Sometimes it covers up a lack of courage.)

Our getting married surely would have been a mistake. In growing up we were also growing apart.

As it turned out, his stay at camp that summer became a catalyst for change. He came back a young man with a new sense of direction for his life – and I wasn't in it.

It had been a wonderful, terrible love affair spanning seven years of loving, growing, fighting, breaking up, and making up, over and over again. We had become more like comfortable, sometimes cranky, old married folks than young lovers. Too used to each other, heady excitement had given way to affection. Except for the occasional sex, we were more like brother and sister. And you don't marry your sister.

The journey had been memorable, however. I wouldn't trade it for anything. My high school years and the three that followed are filled with precious memories of youthful indiscretions and bitter-sweet memories of sexual awakening with someone I loved and trusted.

Nick and I remained close – once I recovered from what was for me a devastating break-up. For a time I thought I would die. But I didn't, of course. His wife and I even became good friends. We spent a few vacations together with our children in years to come. I even learned to ride a small motorcycle while visiting them one day at their home in the country. Another love affair – with the bike, that is – that lasts until today.

*****

Having the opportunity to learn about physical love with someone I trusted and loved when I was young, naive, and impressionable set the groundwork for the person I was to become. I am able to give and receive love honestly and openly today because I had a safe place in which to learn. I learned it was okay to be vulnerable.

It's what you have to risk if you want good, long-lasting man-woman love.

* * * * *

There is a time each year in the fall
When the leaves are gold and red and brown.
The air is crisp and cold
And smells of pumpkins, and sharp, tangy apples . . .
And football

For an instant
I am transported back in time . . .

Back in time to when
I am walking hand in hand
With my forever love
We are wearing sneakers and jeans
And shirts under bulky sweaters

Fallen leaves crunch beneath our feet
As we make our way from the football field
to the school
For another Friday night sock hop in the gym

It only happens once a year
It happens every year

* * * * *

Thank you, dear teenager lover, for making my teens so memorable and for helping me learn how to be a woman.

Sitting on my Porch, Oak Park, MI, Summer 1955

Moonlight Cruise to Bob-Lo Island, Summer 1955

Deboarding Bob-Lo Boat from Detroit Riverfront, Summer 1955

*Lincoln High School
Senior Prom, 1955*

So Says Sarah –

– On Love and Marriage –

Oh, God. Here's a letter I wrote Wayne. I was twenty-two. In recovery from my broken romance with Nick.

Wayne, however, was my best boy buddy. Who knows when we met. Our parents went to the same church from the time we were toddlers. By the time high school rolled around we went to the same school. He dated my best friend for about four years. Nick was his best friend. Every time we broke up with our "true loves," (about every four or five months) we cried on each other's shoulders. And talked. And talked. Never really dated. Just helped each other through those emotionally traumatic times.

I'm remembering a party our church youth group had at my house around 1957. We were all about 17-19 years old. The party was held in our basement rec room. There were records for dancing and snacks for eating. Dancing wasn't exactly encouraged at our church but it wasn't specifically forbidden as in the case of some fundamentalist groups. Nevertheless, some members had strong personal feelings about the subject.

My own parents were more realistic in their understanding and expectations of teenagers. At least one family must have had strong convictions against it because their daughter spent the whole evening upstairs with my parents because we were **dancing** in the basement. Till then, none of us, my parents included, had known she would feel so compromised. We all felt badly for her and tried to coax her to join us. She just couldn't do it. She literally could not bring herself to go downstairs. Where **"the dancing!"** was.

She finally called her folks to come and get her – quite early in the evening. She never did date much. And never married.

* * * * *

What terrible pain and guilt parents project onto our children – and ourselves – when we are so rigidly uncompromising in our beliefs. If we cannot learn to compromise, this world is doomed.

SARAH'S STORY

Compromise does not always mean lowering your standards, sometimes it means respect for someone else's standards.

*****

I remember dancing with Wayne that night. And experiencing that delightful sense of power common to nubile young women, when I realized he had an erection. We were best friends and definitely not romantically involved, but I still felt that heady exhilaration. In retrospect, I know that his arousal had much less to do with me personally than it did the fact that I was young, female, and there!

*****

From the vantage of 32 more years, I must confess regret for never having tried to practice my wanton wiles on this really neat guy who just happened to be one of my best friends. If you ever read this, Wayne, I just want you to know – I wish we had pursued a little romance some time or other. Maybe we would have "Done It." Just for fun! More poignant memories from our tumultuous teens.

*****

(Of course as you now know, my boyfriend and I Did It. And I suspect Wayne and his girlfriend Did It. We just never admitted it).

So here's my letter telling my best boy friend all about the new love in my life. Wayne was attending New York Law School at the time. And has risen up the corporate ladder accordingly ever since. See, I should have slept with him – who knows – I might now being living the life of leisure as a lawyer's wife!

"March 23, 1960

Dear Wayne,
By now you're probably not speaking to me for not writing for so long. I guess your folks – who talked to my folks – probably told

you there's a new light in my life. So my not writing is all his fault. Tuesday was our anniversary – two months. We've seen each other almost every day.

I can finally and truthfully say I've gotten over Nick. There'll always be a special place in my heart where I remember all the things we shared – so many firsts for both of us – but I'm beginning a life with someone new now and my thoughts are too wrapped up in him to dwell on the past. Already Jerry has become my whole life and if the way he acts and treats me is a true indication, he feels the same. I've never been so happy! No two people could be more suited to one another than Jerry and I. Nick and I seemed to "hit against" each other too much. Jerry and I blend together so perfectly I can hardly believe it. It's as though our personalities are molded for one another. We are compatible in every respect.

Here's a little background I know you're dying to hear. (Bear with me, dear friend, for this typical girl "romantic mush". Okay?)

Our first date was on a Tuesday and we went to Aunt Fanny's for dinner (remember that big, old-fashioned Victorian house on Woodward and 13 Mile they converted to a restaurant several years ago?) and then downtown to see "Operation Petticoat". From then till now we haven't missed but one or two nights seeing each other. Man, like WOW from the start!!! We often go bowling on Saturday afternoons since we're both crazy about it. He recently suggested we get on a summer mixed league, too. Sounds like fun.

Remember Jerry Hutchings? He's dating a girl named Judy and we've gone out with them a few times. Jerry Hutchings is sharing living expenses with my Jerry in my Jerry's house. My Jerry's found a buyer: the papers should be finalized this week. I think the two Jerrys plan to rent a flat in Highland Park for awhile. My Jerry wants to buy another house as soon as he is financially able and has already suggested house hunting! (?)

SARAH'S STORY

My Jerry bought a Dodge Dart a few weeks ago. It's white with red and black interior. It's so cool. He traded in his old 57 green and white Chevy. Now he tells me he would have preferred black but got white because I wanted it. Is that devotion, or what?

He comes to church with me pretty regularly and we're taking a class, "Evidences of Christianity," one night a week at North Central Christian College. It's a course designed to prove the existence of God, prove the bible, and explain what our church teaches and why. It's a good class for Jerry because he says he really isn't sure whether he believes in God or not or whether there is life after death.

This then, is our only difference. Jerry's more concerned than me because he believes you shouldn't go into marriage with known differences. He says there's enough of that later. I guess he's right. But of course, I'm an optimist. . . he's a pessimist . . . like you. I think the only real difference is that of "degree". I think it'll all be solved with studying the bible . . . and TIME. He wants to share my beliefs but has too much integrity just to say he does until he really does. I have to admire his honesty. He says even if there is no God or life after death, he thinks people who have strong religious convictions have a peace and contentment that is missing in non-believers. And he's right, of course. But we both realize it's something that can't be pushed. We think it will come in time. So that little problem and the fact that we don't have any money are the only two things preventing us from getting married right away.

I guess this all sounds very rush, rush to you. But I thought it would happen fast if it ever happened again. And it sure did! But I don't mind waiting a few months. We'll just get to know one another better. We both keep saying it seems like we've known each other forever. I can't believe we've only been together two months. After the first hour of our first date I felt completely natural and relaxed with him. It just gets more natural and more easy with each passing day. Do ya think it could be love? (!)

Loving Jerry is the most consuming thing I've ever felt. Just being with him takes my breath away. Looking into his beautiful blue eyes across the table is just too much – I just melt! Stop laughing at me!

Poor Nick wouldn't know me if he could see the way I act with Jerry. I really am a different person. I don't have to work at it, it just seems natural. My love for Nick was a young girl's love – I was selfish, jealous, and sometimes possessive (of course, so was he; just at different times). My love for Jerry is mature. My constant thought is to make him happy – to do things for him. He says I'm fascinating (who, me?) because I'm so mature and womanly one minute and innocent and naive the next (like when he tells me a joke I don't get). [a]

Jerry is the most sensitive person I've ever met. It frightens me because I'm afraid I may hurt him with knowing it. Because he's so sensitive he seems to know exactly what I need and when. He anticipates my thoughts and feelings almost before I do myself. He claims he knows me better than I know myself and I'm beginning to believe him. I keep saying, "So tell me about me". I would really appreciate someone who could explain me to me since I don't fully understand myself yet. [b]

Well, I'm sure you're thoroughly bored with Jerry talk by now. Guess I got carried away.

I hope and pray you'll find a love like this one of these soon days. I've learned it is worth waiting for.

---

[a] If ever there was a "line" guaranteed to excite and entice a young woman's ego, this has gotta be it, right?

[b] Oh, Give me a break! . . . I was only 22. !!

On another matter, congratulations on your wonderful grades!!! (I should make you eat those words of yours. Remember? "Oh, Sarah, I'll never make it. I'm not smart enough. It's way over my head. Oh yes, this time I've really had it!" What does it take to convince you, you idiot, that you're a genius? Develop some confidence for once!

Re your problem with Joyce. I'm not sure I understand but let's talk about it when you get home. Just because I've found "my own true love," please don't think I want to change our friendship. Give me a call when you get home and we'll go out for coffee again. Now that all my problems are solved (hah!) I can devote the entire evening to solving yours! Maybe we can all double one night while you're home.

Well, it's 6:16 p.m. and I'm still at work. I'll really have to hustle to make it to church. Jerry and I are going to the boat show afterwards.

Again, sorry it took me so long to write. I'll do better next time.

Love, Sarah" ,

September 1992 Update

My God, is anyone ever that young? And naive? And dependent? "Explain me to me"? YUK! Little did I know how revealing these attitudes (both his and mine) really were.

Love is wonderful. The second time around . . . or third . . . whenever. But what a price we pay when we don't even know who we are yet? And why didn't M. Scott Peck write his book, "The Road Less Traveled," 30 years sooner. But then, could I have understood what he was saying? Probably not.

So . . .

. . . on with the saga.

— THE WEDDING —

The wedding of Jerry Sullivan and Sarah Barnes took place at the Ferndale Church of Christ in Ferndale, Michigan, on July 9, 1960.

To quote the Women's section of the newspaper where the wedding announcement was printed, "the bride was beautiful in a dress of antique white satin . . ."

Beautiful was not a term I normally thought of to describe myself. I was petite, 5 feet, 2 inches, 97 pounds. And very proud of my 21 inch waist. I had dark, almost black hair and a small oval face with large expressive eyes, which I knew were my best feature. "Dainty," "wholesome," "pixie-face, "innocent looking" were terms used by family and friends in describing my appearance. And until I was well past 40, people who didn't know me well thought I was about 10 years younger than my age. Not exactly appreciated when you're fifteen, but certainly a delightful assessment any time after 35.

But on that day – July 9, 1960 – I really did feel beautiful. Must have been the dress.

Our church building was quite large with seating for about 400-500 people with two long aisles which separated the pews into three sections. Plus a balcony. Although much of that day has remained a vague blur, my memories of walking down that aisle – which seemed endless – with my father to the strains of the traditional wedding march remain distinct. Although it's true my knees were shaking, I loved every minute of that walk and wished it had taken longer! I did truly feel like a princess!

Because of my church's strong position against instrumental music, we did not have a piano or organ in our building. In my congregation, this restriction did not apply to weddings, however, and we rented an organ and organist to play for the wedding.

Walking down that aisle was the best thing about this auspicious occasion as far as I was concerned. Nothing else about the wedding or reception was really what Jerry and I wanted. We had capitulated to the wishes of my mom and dad regarding who should be invited – the entire congregation – which, in turn, affected the type of reception. A sit-down dinner, which Jerry and I would have preferred, was out of the question for 250 people. So we settled for canapes, fancy sandwiches, and punch. Plus a beautiful wedding cake, of course.

It wasn't that my parents were dictatorial about it. They knew I would have preferred a small wedding and supper for family and close friends but they were caught in the trap of tradition. They didn't want to offend anyone – they had belonged to this church for 25 years and it was customary to invite everyone. So we did. Typical of most men, I guess, Jerry didn't care much one way or the other. Maybe because he'd been through all this pomp and circumstance once before.[4] I think he was just anxious to get to the main event later that night.

With regard to the actual service, our wishes were ignored here, too. Maybe I shouldn't say ignored. In planning the service with my minister, we told him we wanted to exchange the "traditional" wedding vows. In his manipulative and authoritarian way – he hadn't been running this church for 25 years for nothing – he agreed to prepare wedding vows of his own that would be similar but not exactly like the traditional vows. "Exactly" was exactly what we wanted, however. We let ourselves be coerced, of course.

* * * * *

Making up his own version of the usual wedding vows was a perfect example of the thinking in my church. **We** were different. **We** were **not** a denomination. **We** were the **one true church**. So

---

[4] I learned Jerry had been married before and had a daughter, almost three years old, after we had been dating about three months. "So *that's* why he owns a house." By then, we were seriously involved.

of course we couldn't do anything – including repeating wedding vows – like any one else. Theoretically speaking, if people in other churches entered through the door – **we** would use the window!

Our congregation was so different, in fact, that we didn't even agree with most other churches within our own religion. (Denomination is the correct word here, but I can't say it because, as I told you, we weren't – a denomination, that is). The not-so-subtle implication was that our congregation was the true champion of **THE WORD**. Disagreeing with our teaching relative to wine (Biblical) versus grape juice (**not** Biblical) in the Lord's Supper and selection of elders (**not** Biblical), in particular, were matters of grave concern and members were admonished against getting too friendly with congregations who differed from us in their teaching about these issues. If your eternal soul is at stake, you take such matters seriously.

*****

Nevertheless, given the restrictions placed upon us by our "traditions," still it was a lovely wedding and if there were any "hitches" (no pun intended) I was blissfully unaware of them.

After the church reception, family and a few close friends were asked to accompany us back to my parents' home. I trust the others were not offended. After a change of clothing and a few brief pleasantries, Jerry and I headed off for the "main event," which took place in a nice hotel somewhere in the metropolitan Detroit area, (in the vicinity of 14 Mile/Woodward) accompanied by the expected lacy bedroom attire and a bottle of champagne, most of which was emptied into the sink the next morning.

I wish I could remember all the exciting details of that momentous occasion but I don't. I do remember we "did it" four times!

* * * * *

One reason the details of that night aren't embedded in my brain may be because it was **not** the night I lost my virginity. As mentioned earlier, that had happened five years earlier with my teenage lover.

Neither was it the first time Jerry and I made love. But since ours was a whirlwind romance – we knew each other six months before our marriage – the opportunities for sin were relatively short-lived.

* * * * *

We left the next morning for a week's stay at a cottage at Houghton Lake, Michigan. Again, the details remain illusive. We were young, we were in love, and acted accordingly. I do remember counting how many times we "did it" all during that week and for several weeks after returning to our duplex where we set up housekeeping. I got up to number 84 before I lost track!

* * * * *

Years later, as I was trying desperately to cling to the positive, valid tenets of my religion, to play or not to play – the church organ, that is – became a catalyst of change for me philosophically.

Since the early years of our marriage, I had been trying to see my church through the eyes of my husband to better understand his point of view. The more I put myself in his place, the more valid his criticism seemed. It is nearly impossible to reject "**the one true church**", however.

By this time we had three small children. Because I didn't want to create confusion for them, I continued to send them to Sunday School by bus, which a nearby congregation provided. Sometimes I followed an hour later for worship service, sometimes I didn't.

One particular Sunday, however, I was very much in need of "spiritual food" and drove off to church accordingly. It was a typical service – typical songs, typical sermon. Unfortunately, I was in need of something untypical. But didn't get it. Hadn't been getting it for some time. Which may have been my fault, rather than theirs.

During a lapse in my attention to the service, I began reading their weekly bulletin. A few lines in a church bulletin. Such a small thing, really, but such an impact it made. Like the straw that broke the camel's back.

A wedding was planned and apparently the family had asked permission to use an organ. The decision was printed in the bulletin along with the general invitation. "Because we do not believe in the use of instrumental music, the elders have decided it would not be appropriate for an organ to be brought in for the wedding service. Tape recorded music will be offered instead."

I had gone to church that day starving for spiritual nourishment. But my plate was not filled. Reading that notice made it clear to me WHY. A church concerned about the distinction between a mechanical reproduction of an organ (spiritually acceptable) versus a real live organ (spiritually unacceptable) could not possibly address my spiritual needs.

Reading that announcement, the apron strings were forever severed. From that time on, I seriously began to look elsewhere for a belief system that would fill up my spiritual plate whenever it was empty.

Marriage and Parenthood

Sarah Barnes

Jerry Sullivan

And Two Become One . . .

The Most Beautiful Kids in the World Club . . .

Tom, One Year

John, 18 Months

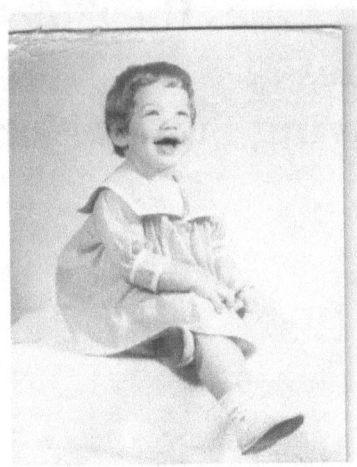

Caryn Jo, One Year

Lisa Danielle (Pie)
One Year

THE FANTASY

**Tick-Tock Tick-Tock Goes the Clock
Time Flies . .
(Whether You're Having Fun or Not)**

Suddenly it's . . .

SARAH'S STORY

December 1971

Merry Christmas!

Look who's trying to write a Xmas letter! (Sarah has her hands full with the wild bunch, hence no letter last year. (*)

We have had a busy year, but as usual nothing spectacular. Sarah and I got away (by ourselves) for a three-day weekend to Dayton, Ohio, courtesy of my sister, Linda, who babysat. We just loafed and ate and generally had a good time.

We also spent a week at the lake with our friends Nick and Jenny Dalton. Also, I took the two boys up north to Dad and Mom's new house and they had a hellava time catching frogs and snakes while I painted. I enjoyed it too. It's very peaceful there at Forrest Lake. They have the outside complete now and are going to start finishing the inside this Spring.

The kids are Tom, 8 years; John, six; Caryn, four; and Dani (short for Danielle), fifteen months. They are all well and healthy. Tom and John are doing well in school (at least grade-wise). The two boys and I are in Indian Guides and really enjoy it. We go on about five weekend camp-outs a year and meet twice a month. We have a project or field trip planned for each meeting. The worst punishment for them is to miss a meeting, but I seldom invoke it.

Caryn is going to Nursery School and taking ballet lessons and is quite a Lady. She is one of the bright spots in my life and has learned that if she gets up on my lap, gives me a hug and kiss, and says, "I Love You, Daddy," that I'll give her the world.

Dani is the terror. The only time she's not in trouble is when en route from the mess she just made to the one she's going to make. I think she takes after her mother.

Speaking of Sarah, she is fine and busy, naturally, and has learned to Knit and Crochet and spends the evening hours making things for the kids. Damn! I wish she would come to bed sometime.

So all things considered, it has been a good year. We are looking forward to the Holidays and expect to have a Merry Christmas.

We send you our best wishes for a Merry Christmas and a Happy New Year.

Love,The Sullivan Family

(*) Working part-time evenings at Sears and filling in occasionally as Room Mother kept me plenty busy. This year, Jer's first at writing what had become our "year in the life of" Christmas letters, was so well received he continued to do so for the next several years much to the delight of family and friends. His sense of humor and "turn of phrase," so different from my own, was justly appreciated.

SARAH'S STORY

Christmas 1975

Ho-Ho-Ho!

Just got the bills paid for last Christmas so it must be time to compose another cherry greeting. Time really flies nowadays. They tell me that's a sign of old age. I couldn't say but will take their word for it.

The Great Spirit has been good to us again this year. Tom is now 12 and almost as big as Sarah and needs braces. John, 10, is still smiling, taking violin lessons, and needs braces. Both boys are into the normal boy things; rockets, airplanes, baseball, football, and trouble. Caryn, 8, is still my lover, a Brownie, and still taking gymnastics and doing very well in school. Dani, 5, lives in her own world which I can seldom penetrate (she tells me she is doing fine and is madly in love with the little boy across the street). Sarah, age deleted, is still happily working at Sears and needs braces (or crowns, bridge-work, or something).

I am very busy at work. It gets hectic at times but never boring. Finally get to travel a bit with two trips to southern California and two to New York City this year. Also got to see Ellen[5] while out West. She is 19, in her second year of college, working part-time, and very pretty.

As a family, we still enjoy riding our motorcycles. We have six running and a parts bike. Sarah and I hope to take a week's camping trip on them soon, hopefully next summer. (Just the two of us). We are just waiting our acceptance into "Hells Angels". Understand Sarah has to grow a beard to pass.

In the meantime, she has discovered house plants. They are all over the place. She talks to them all the time and calls them by name. I'm not sure what she's telling them but the three biggest ones have tried to strangle me so far.

---

[5] Jer's daughter from his first marriage.

Sarah has long been a booster of southern hospitality (Tennessee style) but after a week in South Dakota this summer she's also a believer in the South Dakota kind. Thanks to Cousin Pam and Aunts Alice, Lois, and Pat. We really had a good time. Grandma Sullivan is as pretty and sharp as ever.

I've been told my letters lack the religious aspect expected in Christmas letters, so to correct this I am asking you all to pray. . . for dental insurance.

Wishing you all the best —
Love from The Sullivans

SARAH'S STORY

Christmas 1978

Merry Christmas to all you good people. Hope this finds you all healthy and happy. Wealthy too, if that's your wish. We have survived another year without any major difficulties.

Both Sarah's folks and mine have retired and moved away this year. Mine up North and hers down South. So we have two more places to go for a free vacation. We miss them already.

Sarah just received her five-year pin from Sears. The kids and I received a purple heart for five years of eating spaghettios and tomato soup beyond the call of duty. I also received a pin and an appointment with the Psychiatrist for staying at Burroughs for 25 years. He called me a Masochist. Whatever that is.

As for the kids:

Tom, the oldest at 15, is dreaming of cars and girls and is not sure what to do with either. (We hope).

John, 13, is trying to horn in on Tom's dreams and also fancies himself as a young Tom Edison. Caryn, 11, is one of those damn 'perfect kids' but I'll catch her at something yet.

Lisa, 8, is a pretty little thing but I can't figure her out beyond that. (Just like her mother, I guess.)

Ellen is coming here for a week in January. (After too many years, though, I did get out there twice this year.) She is 22, working and going to college.

We enjoyed trips to South Dakota, Tennessee, and up North this year for reunions, play, etc.

We built a deck on the house this year after redoing the kitchen, finishing the basement, and building a garage in the last two years. We now have the place about the way we want it. You guessed it. We have decided it's time to move and are looking. (Too soon old and too late smart).

Other than that we stay busy with just living day-to-day trying to do the best we can.

Merry Christmas, Happy New Year and Much Love
from The Sullivans

The Beginning Of . . .

Christmas 1979

Dear Friends and Family,

We sincerely hope this note finds you healthy, happy, and prosperous.

Well, we have survived another year doing the best we can. No V.P.'s, doctors or scholarships in the family; however, we are all working our way through the school of hard knocks.

Ellen now lives in San Diego, still in college working towards her degree in Computer Science.

Tom, 16, is a typical teenager, dammit. Has a girl friend and is teaching himself to play the electric guitar. (This time please pray for a power failure.).

John, 14, never quits smiling and swears he will be a millionaire by age 25. (Didn't think there was that much money in custom garbage picking).

Caryn, 12, is pretty, sweet, a good student, plays the flute, and has kidney trouble (flares up whenever there are dishes to be washed).

Lisa, 9, is also pretty, and very independent. Typical youngest of the family (no further comment needed).

Sarah, 39 and holding, is still with Sears and active in the church, sings in the choir (bass, I think).

Me, I'm still the same composed, steady, honest, and loveable old self. Also unemployed. Resigned from Burroughs after 26 years. I have a job pending in northeastern Tennessee and am hoping for the best.

As I write this greeting, Sarah and I are preparing to leave for Tennessee – in the morning – December 10th – to look for a house and to further explore job possibilities.

Anyway, 1980 will be very eventful for us. Your prayers on our behalf will be very much appreciated. Our prayers for you are, as always, that the new year will be everything you wish it to be.

MERRY CHRISTMAS AND HAPPY NEW YEAR TO ALL.
Love from The Sullivans

12/20   P.S. Our new address, at least from January 15 – July 15 is:
1407 Lake Drive Extension, Johnson City, TN 37601

December 20, 1980

Merry Christmas to "Ya'll" from the Sunny South!

Well, dear ones, our sincerest holiday greetings come to you this year from Franklin, Tennessee (25 miles south of Nashville).

It's been an eventful year for us. We moved to Johnson City, Tennessee, in January. It was a beautiful area at the edge of the Smokies but wages were very low. So in June we bought a business in Nashville known as Delamotte-Turner of Nashville. It is an apartment refurbishing company, which means we paint, clean, and steam clean carpets for apartment complexes. We do some of the work ourselves, when necessary, but mostly I supervise the workers and Sarah supervises me, in addition to keeping the books.

After 20 years of messing up my checkbook I dreaded letting her near the books but she does an excellent job and is much more thorough than I would be. Her dad has been invaluable also in lending his expertise (he's a retired accountant) in getting us started on the right track. And by visiting every 4-5 weeks he helps us stay there. Business is up and down like a yo-yo. It is frustrating and rewarding in the same way but I think we'll make it. (Call us when your toilet needs cleaning).

The move to Johnson City was hard on the kids after living in one house all their lives but they took the second move better and have made some friends and seem to be adjusting well.

Lisa, 10 (we call her "busy butt") has boundless energy, takes piano lessons, has a different boy friend each week, and can work circles around the rest of us.

Caryn, 13, still plays the flute (first chair at last), plays basketball, and plays for time (whenever there are dirty dishes). We kid her that everything in her room is either gray or green. Gray is dust; green is food. She points out, though, that we can't even check the boys' rooms because of the stench from tennis shoes and dirty socks!

But Lisa is smart – she sleeps with Caryn whenever she can get away with it – so her room is usually neat as a pin!

John, 15, also has excess energy (2 out of 4 ain't bad). He's always "fixing" something or making something, and helps me fix cars. Think he has some of Grandpa Sullivan's talent in this regard.

Tom, 17, had the toughest time adjusting but is doing great now; trying hard to keep tabs on a little girl back in Michigan. He works at Goose Creek Inn (restaurant), is forming a rock band for which he plays lead guitar, and gets straight A's in "Automotive Reasoning" (that's the development of reasons to use the car).

Ellen lives near San Diego now and is finishing college, working, and dieting. (She tells me she inherited the Sullivan "fat leg" curse from me).

Sarah bowls (?) in addition to running the business and is becoming a Southern Belle. I do think bowling in a hoop skirt, bonnet, and parasol is a bit much, though.

Me, I run around taking people to lunch whenever possible and try to find time to restore a 1960 Thunderbird we bought in Johnson City. I heard you could always tell a <u>rich</u> Southern gentleman by the two junk cars he has up on blocks in the front yard. So I give them something to think about with <u>four.</u> Now let them try and call me a Damn Yankee! (Everything is ok, though, when I tell them I'm from **South** Dakota).

All in all, we are well and happy. We took a big chance and the jury is still out but we are trying hard and hoping for the best. Sarah says with me drumming up the business, her handling the books, and the Lord holding it all together, we can't miss. Hope she's right.

The hardest part was leaving all our friends and relatives. We miss you all and hope this year and next is everything you wish them to be.

Love from The Sullivans and . . .
Ya'll Come

December 1981

A Very Merry Christmas and a Happy New Year to All You Good People (Ya'll)

This is our second Christmas in the great state of Tennessee and we're starting our second year of self-employment. We've learned a lot since starting this new venture and I suppose we still have more to learn. However, we eat well and if the IRS will let us keep any of our earnings, then we can consider the year a successful one.

The family has become acclimated to southern living for the most part. Especially the female half. The boys and I aren't so sure but are making the best of it. Sometimes it seems we have the same old problems in a new location. The car that only acts up when Sarah has it (she seems to think it pertinent that I add she's the one who drives it 97% of the time), the toilet that starts running at 2 a.m., and the septic tank that backs up if more than two people shower consecutively. I guess that's life.

While we have many new friends we all do miss the old friends and relatives more than we can say.

As for us. Lisa, 11, plays the piano, basketball, baseball, is in Girl Scouts, and changes boyfriends more often than the boys change their socks. Caryn, 14, is a high school freshman (or fresh person, whatever is proper now). It seems she is always gone these days to some function or other. She is in Marching Band and is proud of getting second chair in the flute section in her first year. (Tries out for All-State Band this weekend). John, 16, is perpetually busy tinkering. He worked with me every day this summer and bought a convertible with his earnings. He was King S--T when he was the only kid in Drivers' Ed with his own wheels (never mind he couldn't drive without an adult). Tom, 18, graduated from high school this year and is also working in the business; painting and steaming carpets while he decides his life's vocation, which changes

SARAH'S STORY

every week. He also plays a mean guitar. He plans to attend college but not at this time (our accountant applauds this decision).

Ellen, 25, graduated this month in San Diego with a degree in Business and Computer Science. At this time she is considering several job offers (including Burroughs, which I find somewhat ironic).

Sarah still does all the business paper work and has also named herself "President of the Treasury" and otherwise keeps busy with church, bowling, and school activities.

Me – I feel like I'm working my butt off, but it's as big as ever. Anyhow, stay busy working on cars and equipment, cutting firewood, playing cards once a week with the guys (neighbors), bowling, and even tried deer hunting this year (no, I didn't get one).

As a family we didn't get away for a summer vacation this year though Sarah and the girls made a two-week trip to Michigan at the end of June. (Yep, you guessed it, she did have car trouble). We do plan a quick trip to Michigan over Christmas. I must add we are all disappointed in the decrease in visitors this year (though we do thank our parents, the Cains, Papadelises, Yonkeys, Ruth Huber, and the Wests for brightening our doorstep). There's lots to see here and while I can't promise to take time off, we sure will try to make you welcome and give you a map showing the points of interest. The World's Fair will be opening in Knoxville in the spring and that's just a half-day drive from here so maybe that'll entice some of you.

In closing, we wish you all the very best of everything this Christmas season and throughout the coming year.

All our Love,
The Sullivans

. . . The End . . .

SARAH'S STORY

December 20, 1982

Dear Friends,

Well, I'm really late getting things done this year. Waited so long to buy cards that this podunky little town hasn't got any left. Can you imagine?! (But I love this little podunky town anyway.) So this letter will have to serve as my Christmas card to ya'll.

I guess by now most of you know that Jerry sold the business and accepted a job back in Michigan with Burroughs. We've had the house up for sale since July but as we all know houses just aren't moving. So don't know when we'll be moving back. Tom went with Jerry and they both are coming down for a quick four-day trip. At least Tom will be coming if he can get someone to work for him on Christmas weekend, which doesn't seem likely.

In the interim I got myself a job, which I'm enjoying very much, though, as indicated above, it really keeps me busy and a little more behind schedule than my usual 3-4 day lag. I'm secretary to the president of Matrix Enterprises, Inc., an MSO cable company. MSO means multi-system organization. Which, in turn, means that we are the corporate office for 15 cable systems in the Tennessee-Kentucky and Illinois and Ohio area. Naturally, they are seeking to expand at every opportunity but will be confined to those four states for some time, I'm sure. I'm sure learning a lot – and believe me, folks, that TV of ours is going to be more and more a central part of our lives in the next few years. And cable TV is going to be a big part of those innovations.

Caryn, as always, is enjoying school and band very much. She got first chair flute this year so we're all happy about that too. Lisa started middle school and joined sixth grade band playing the clarinet (we steered her to that instrument) but kept bugging me to switch her to the trumpet. So at the end of the two-month rental period, we let her switch. She got the trumpet on Monday evening and played it so long that first night her lip got swollen. By the end of the week she had caught up to the band, which amounted to six weeks worth of study. I just hope her enthusiasm continues. Caryn is a good example, though, and inspiration, I hope. She plans to major in music and is naturally hoping for some kind of scholarship. Mom thinks that's a good idea too, of course.

John is totally happy here in Tennessee. At last. Mostly because he's become best friends with a little girl named Kim. She happens to be Jessie Carter's[1] daughter and they live just about a mile away. They both <u>insist</u> they're just good friends but I'm beginning to doubt it. However, at this point, John is ready to be anything she wants him to be.

The most exciting thing for him is the fact that they just invited him to go on a Caribbean Cruise with them. Several months ago they had planned this cruise and contracted for ten people to go, mostly her band and their wives plus a friend or two. Jessie was to perform 2-3 shows as part of the deal. Anyway, at the last minute, one of the men who was going mostly to help Ben (Jessie's husband) drive the bus to and from Florida was unable to go. So guess who they invited to take his place??? The lucky little S--T! They left on November 27th and came back on the 5th, being on the boat from Sunday to Sunday.

Well, as usual, I've just told you everything you never wanted to know about the adventures of the Sullivan family, and have run out of space in the process.

I think of you often and always ask God to bless you and keep you in His care. I've been moving towards this for the past few years and think I'm at the point where frequently I can relax and be content to be wherever I am, doing whatever I'm doing, because I know

---

[1] Fictitious name of country singer.

God is working everything out for my and my family's good. Even during the times when it seems just the opposite.(*)

I hope you have the same kind of peace and acceptance.

And have a very happy holiday season and I hope God heaps tons of blessing on you in the coming year.

Love from the Sullivans

XXX XXXXXXX XXXX
Franklin, TN 37064
615-XXX-XXX

(*) Most everyone who got this letter probably understood this was my way of referencing the awful tragedy taking place in our family – the pending separation and divorce – otherwise covered up in this sugar-coated annual summation of a year in the life of The Sullivans.

THE REALITY

The tragedy . . .

. . . was that this family, after struggling for twenty-two years to survive, was finally and irrevocably breaking apart.

Jerry's return to Michigan with Tom was planned. He told me he was moving back to Michigan . . . and a job at Burroughs . . . one Friday night in September of 1982. He made it clear he was returning without me. I knew for several months he had been planning something drastic but he hadn't said anything and I hadn't asked. The only thing I wasn't sure about was when.

After his announcement – he took me out for dinner that night – he asked, "what are you going to do?"

I was kind of in a state of shock . . . but I wasn't. If that makes sense. There was a deep cold calm in the pit of my stomach. It was not pleasant but it was not panic either.

"I don't know, actually. I think we both have realized for the past couple of years this day was coming. I don't know what I'll do. Actually. We will survive. I will survive. How, I don't know. Yet."

— And That Was . . .

The End of the Beginning —

A few weeks later Jerry left. Tom left with him; he had graduated high school that summer and had kept in touch with many of his friends from Michigan, including a former girl friend, so I could understand why he wanted to return.

The rest of us; John, Caryn, Lisa and I did what we had to do.

And the first thing we had to do was move.

Because we had used our funds from the sale of our home in Michigan in 1980 to start our business in Tennessee, we were unable to get a mortgage when we moved to Franklin. We did manage to get a two-year land contract on a house, thinking we would have money for a down payment at the end of that time. The contract was now up and the remaining Sullivans had to leave.

The owners had no sympathy for our circumstances and gave me short notice to vacate their premises. I managed to find a house to rent a few miles away. Somehow John and his friends and Caryn managed to move our furniture into a rented van which John drove to our new home. When I say "furnishings" I am including a player piano, a floor freezer chest, a washer and dryer – extremely heavy items – as well as the usual home furnishings from a five-bedroom home with family room. Somehow they managed to move everything out of one house and into another. How I will never know; mostly I was at work.

Two months after renting the house in the country, the owners advised they wanted their mother to live there so we moved again. To a three-bedroom apartment across from Franklin High School.

This required transferring the kids from the county to city schools. John was mostly not attending school, period. He frequently stayed overnight at the Carter's; I could not convince Jessie to send him home at a reasonable hour. Considering the fact that I turned to him for help every time he turned around I can't blame him. In the first two months after Jerry left, every thing that could break did. The frig, the car, the washer, the dryer. On and on it went. No wonder he stayed away!

Caryn struggled at her school for a semester and then moved back to Michigan with her father for her senior year of high school. My youngest, Lisa, had also switched from the county middle school to the city middle school. It was a difficult transition for her, as well. In the summer of that same year, she moved back to Michigan with her sister and father. She was just shy of her fourteenth birthday. I carry with me always the pain of losing the mothering experiences I missed with her at a time when she needed them most.

Although John never finished his last year of high school, he and Kim got married in the fall of 1984. Immediately he began running Sound for Jessie. Eventually he got his GED and spent the next ten years as Jessie's sound engineer, eventually becoming a well-respected Sound Man in the music industry. Down time was spent in construction. His innate intelligence, ability to problem-solve, and sense of responsibility enabled him to succeed at both vocations. Which has continued to the present.

Life goes on. Somehow. We cave or survive. I survived. We all survived. Somehow. After the first couple of years, it was even possible for me to stay at the house Jerry was renting in Royal Oak on the few occasions I managed to afford a trip to Michigan to see the kids.

By 1985 I was working full-time and managing to pay the bills, mostly. From the time Jerry left til then, my life had consisted of work and home and sometimes church. Finally I knew it was time to begin looking for some kind of social outlet. I heard of a support group of single parents and started attending the monthly meetings.

— Sarah In The Middle ---

This is about the woman, Sarah, now middle-aged, and then some. And what came next.

The saga continues.

— Yes, Virginia, I mean Sarah, There Is Life After Divorce --

For two years after Jerry left, I lived like a hermit, emotionally dead.

Mark woke me up.

This required some soul-searching. After which I made a decision – I decided sleeping with another single adult would no longer be a moral issue. For me. And because consistency and logic are important to me in problem solving and forming opinions, I had to take this to its logical conclusion which meant that, one or 20, it doesn't matter. Hmmmm.

My girls had gone to live with their dad in the spring and summer of 1984. Shortly thereafter, I realized that going to work, coming home, fixing dinner, watching TV, and repeating the process daily was not a healthy way to live. I needed some kind of balance. I joined Parents Without Partners shortly thereafter and agreed to become an officer in the local chapter. We planned weekly activities for the adults and one or two family-style activities each month. Since my children were gone, I concentrated on attending the adult activities. It was good to get out and know that I had a group of friends waiting at a pre-appointed destination.

Mark was a surprise. He was ten years younger than me and I perceived his interest to be based on the fact that we were both displaced Yankees. We met for drinks and dancing one evening. Later, when he walked me to my car, I was completely taken off guard by his goodnight kiss – and totally surprised at the intense physical reaction I felt.

I figured he was just being polite or doing what he thought was expected. Except I hadn't been expecting it. I had become comfortable with the realization that PWP had given me a group of adults, men and women, who did things together as friends. Romantic liaisons were not assumed or expected.

There had been no sex between Jerry and I – no affection of any kind – for about two years before he left us and moved back to Michigan in the fall of 1982. I had become accustomed to functioning more like a robot than a human being. Sexual urges were few and far between and I had always been adept at satisfying those urges partner or not. I thought my emotional and physical feelings towards a man were dead and gone.

What a shock I got that night in the parking lot. I spent the next several months rediscovering what it's like to live with an almost insatiable pit of desire burning in my gut. Even talking with this man on the phone produced it. Eventually we ended up in bed, of course. But always we were more friends than lovers. And I was too self-conscious about the intensity of my feelings. I knew it was purely physical but this was my first experience in more than four years and I felt self-conscious about encouraging or talking to him about the proper ways to satisfy a woman. He was so much younger and hadn't had a great deal of experience. Typically female, I didn't want to bruise his ego. So our bedroom antics merely added fuel to the fire under the tea in my kettle that was rising to the boiling point.

I dated and bedded about three other men before I met Scott.

It was always just for fun and to "catch up" for what I thought I'd missed. None of them were serious relationships. Because we all understood this, we were able to remain friends afterwards. It's kind of like having a warm spot in your heart for someone you had lunch with. These kinds of relationships would have been impossible in my "other" life, of course. And rightly so.

So this was a whole new ball game for me. The turf is different, the rules are different too. Hopping from bed to bed has become a rite of passage for men and women in our society, for good or bad, and certainly not unusual for someone who is trying to find his/her path after a divorce.

Right or wrong – having decided that single adults sleeping with other single adults was no longer a moral issue for me, the number of times and who and when I did it became irrelevant. If it's wrong, it's wrong. If it's okay, one or twenty, men or times, it doesn't matter. In fact, the more, the better.

Several months later when Scott came to dinner that first time, I was the one to suggest we adjourn to my bedroom! Little did he know then that the tea in the kettle was ready to spout! We were sitting, then lying on the couch, making out just like a couple of teenagers. I was trying to act like a sophisticated, mature woman of the world (the 80's world). He told me sometime later that it kind of surprised him but, like most men in that situation, he wasn't about to turn down the offer. (Men – they're always ready, willing and able, aren't they?) He thought it would happen. Just not that soon. Nor without some affectionate coaxing on his part.

Fortunately for me, Scott was well-acquainted with the female anatomy. Being a bachelor for 12 years he'd had plenty of time to perfect his technique. That night we entered into a wonderfully exciting and fulfilling physical relationship that continued for several years. Of course, we're weren't up there on the mountaintop all the time like we were for the first six months or so – but when we made the climb, it's was always worth it.

New Ethic, New Life, New Love

December 26, 1985

Dear Friends,

Although I didn't get my act together enough to send out any Christmas cards, I will try to get this in the mail before the holidays are completely over.

I've been terrible about writing letters this year and I haven't heard from too many of you, either. Maybe that's because I moved again – so be sure and note my new address. I had the chance to buy a mobile home last Spring – not as financially prudent as buying a house but still better than renting year after year. So I expect to stay put for a good long while.

It's really nice – 80 x 14, 3-bedroom, 2 baths – and located in a nice park. John and Kim are just down the street. Even though the park is located in the city limits of Franklin, we're surrounded by hills so it's kind of like being out in the country.

This has really been a year of change and growth (I hope) for me in lots of ways. Mostly good, I think. I've learned that I **AM** a survivor and that being alone doesn't have to mean being lonely. That's a neat thing to learn. The only hard part is being away from Lisa, Caryn, and Tom. But I feel good knowing Jerry is willing and able to take care of them. He calls often to keep me informed, which I really appreciate.

In some respects my life has taken a 180 degree turn – but basically I'm still the same old (poor choice of words) me. I've enclosed a little poem I came across in a church bulletin several months ago. It's message seemed to reach out and grab me and it pretty well expresses my outlook at this stage of my life (I'm just glad I came across it before I got to be 85!).

Being single and free does have its rewards. I have time to do things just for me – and that's nice. I'm trying to reawaken my brain

– though much of the time I'm frustrated in this endeavor and feel as though too much of it has gone to seed and is irretrievable – but I'm tryin'.

Last January I met a really nice man and we have spent all or part of every weekend since together (no raised eyebrows, please, or friendly advice, either, thanks. I get enough of that from Caryn and John!) He's 5'8", 140 lbs., medium brown hair, blue eyes, attractive. He was married for 4 years and has been single for 12 and since I was married for 22 years and single for 3, we've come to some similar conclusions for somewhat different reasons, mainly that nothing lasts forever. So we're just hangin' out together and having lots of fun for however long it lasts. We claim to be Nashville's oldest living teenagers.

I guess we're both "late bloomers". He was over 35 when he went back to college and over 40 when he bought his first motorcycle (you know I'd find **someone** who likes motorcycles) and we spent the spring and summer tooling around Nashville and Surrounds on his Harley-Davidson 1340 Super Glide.

Another fun thing we do is go to Drag Races. He has a 1967 Buick GranSport which he sometimes races. We took it out on one of our country back roads a few months ago; he showed me how to "rev" it up, and then he dropped it into gear for me and told me to "hit it" – so I "hit it". . . and went from 0 to 90 in about 6 seconds. After I picked myself up off the floor of the back seat and caught my breath, I was OK. His best racing time on the track (so far) is 13.6 in the quarter mile – which is pretty good for a "street rod". He also belongs to the Buick Club of America and we've had some fun times with them, too. (Buicks are THE ONLY car, you know!)

I realize this sounds more like a star-struck teenager in love than a mature 47-year-old woman . . .

So what.

Although my present job is ending December 31st, I'm optimistically looking forward to a better job and more money – hopefully my expectations will not go unrewarded.

John and Kim drove to Michigan on December 15th and I rode the bus up last Sunday evening and stayed with Jerry and the girls. John and Kim and I drove back late Christmas Day and they have now gone on to Texas for a Christmas with Kim's grandparents.

Guess that brings you up to date. Plus I've run out of space. I hope this past year has been a good one for all of you and that the new year will be filled with health and happiness for each of you. Please write or visit sometime and let me know what's going on with each of you.

Love, Sarah
P.S. I've enclosed a copy of the poem – you're probably familiar with it.

IF I Had My Life To Live Over
by Nadine Stair, 85 years old, Louisville, KY

If I had my life to live over,
I'd dare to make more mistakes next time.
I'd relax, I would limber up.
I would be sillier than I have been this trip.
I would take fewer things serious.
I would take more chances.
I would climb more mountains and swim more rivers.
I would eat more ice cream and less beans.
I would perhaps have more actual troubles,
but I'd have fewer imaginary ones.

You see, I'm one of those people who live sensibly
   and sanely hour and hour, day after day.
Oh, I've had my moments, and if I had it to do over again,
   I'd have more of them.
In fact, I'd try to have nothing else.
Just moments, one after another,
Instead of living so many years ahead of each day.

I've been one of those persons who never goes
   anywhere without a thermometer, a hot water bottle,
   a raincoat and a parachute.
If I had to do it again,
I would travel lighter than I have.

If I had my life to live over,
I would go to more dances.
I would ride more merry-go-rounds,
I would pick more daisies.

December 24, 1986

Ho, Ho, Ho!

'Tis the night before Christmas and here I am writing a last minute epistle to enclose with my last minute cards. But then, it's nice to know some things never change, right?

I hope you all have a nice Christmas and that Santa brings you health and peace of mind in the coming year. If only there really was a Santa who could bring peace and happiness to the whole world. Instead there's just ordinary folks like you and me, doing the best we can one day at a time.

So here I am, doing what I can to deal with every day situations; some good, some bad. Having heard from a few of you lately, I know I'm not alone in this. But you can't live to be our age without experiencing some heartaches along the way. Hopefully, we gain strength and courage along the way. And adversity **does** teach us to appreciate the good times, right? Right!!.

And I have had my share of good times this year.

Scott and I are still having fun – whenever we can (which is most of the time). I've just put my mobile home up for sale and plan to move to Nashville once it sells. A 45-minute drive to and from work each day is not **too** much fun. I'll send a change of address once I get resettled (not that it will do much good since most of you are not that good at writing anymore).

I think I told you previously that my son John and his wife Kim live in a mobile home in the same park as I do. They spend most of their time traveling on the "Jessie Bus," of course, but this is a slow time of year for them so they just made a quick trip to Michigan for Christmas with their Michigan family (John's dad and his family). My folks left yesterday for Michigan, also. They had planned to come here but my brother had an emergency appendectomy last week and is still very sick fighting the poisons in his system so they wanted to be with him. John and Kim are back home for a few days and will spent Christmas with me and then go on to Texas to be with Kim's grandparents.

You may not know that my son Tom and his girlfriend Josie recently moved down here. They are staying temporarily with Kim and John but are planning on moving into an apartment soon. Also soon, I am to be a grandmother. And another soon, they will get married. Seems like the order got switched around a little, but what do I know, I'm still trying to adjust to being a grandmother! Besides, I'm in no position to judge.

Caryn (19) and Lisa (16) are still living with their dad. Caryn has a nice boyfriend, I understand, and she divides her time between him, work, and part-time school (unfortunately in that order, I believe). Lisa, as usual, is attempting to be about 3-5 years older than she is and has temporarily moved out (I say "temporarily" hopefully) and just comes back to visit. She dropped out of school and is working and planning to go to a vocational school in Royal Oak. Caryn tried this a couple of years ago – moving out, that is – but moved back with her dad after a couple of weeks. Lisa, being more stubborn and headstrong may need more time. But at least they are all talking from time to time so I guess that's the best we can hope for right now. Who said, "These are the times that try men's souls"? He **was** talking about raising kids, wasn't he?

On the whole, this has been a good year for me and I expect 1987 to be even better. I hope you are looking forward to the new year, too, and want to extend my wishes that it will be one of mental and spiritual growth and physical well-being for you and your families. Sometimes we just gotta "hang in there".

Even though none of us write much anymore, you are all still special to me and I hope you know the welcome lamp is lit if you're ever in the Sunny South.

Shalom, Sarah

Spring 1987

THE STRAY(*)

I call her "Annie Roonie'
Or sometimes, "Orphan Annie"

My neighbor had taken pity on her
nine years ago when, as a stray,
she came begging at her door

Now my neighbor was moving away
and asked if I would take over
the care and feeding of the little cat

She'd been stopping at my door
for nearly two years now anyway
to get a meal or two from time to time
when my neighbor wasn't home
so I said "yes, of course"

Everything was fine for two weeks
Miss Annie just came more often
for her meals and daily dose of affection

Then new neighbors moved in

A female boxer with six pups
took up residence
she charged and barked
every time we came outdoors

Annie Rooney disappeared

For days at a time I didn't see her
then she'd appear in the back yard
or on the front steps looking
forlorn and mewing pathetically

Always keeping a safe distance
from the side door where
she used to take her meals

My heart went out to the little stray
as I imagined her confusion
first her people leave
and now she can't go home

And where is home anyway?

Like any cat who's survived
nine years on the street
eventually she adapted

Lately she's even taken
to scratching at the front door
and calling out in cat talk
to make her presence known

I sit on the steps with her
and wait as she eats

She takes a bite or two of food
then turns to me and shoves
her nose up under my hand
for the petting and caressing
she wants and needs

as much as she needs the food
The process is repeated several times

I am touched by the way
her two front paws knead
back and forth like a kitten
when it suckles from its mother
as I rub her head and chin
and murmur softly in her ear.

(*) This little stray cat started stopping by which prompted me to write this poem

SARAH'S STORY

December 15, 1987

Merry Christmas!

Old habits die hard and I can't seem to break the one that says I need to write yet another Christmas missive. Partly due to the fact that many of these relationships have resolved themselves down to Christmas only communications – I'm just not ready to let go altogether. Are you? Good, then here goes.

Please note my address change indicated at the bottom of the letter. I moved from Franklin last January. I am presently employed at J. C. Bradford & Co. (the largest brokerage firm in the Southeast – just because YOU never heard of it – hmmmph!). I've been here since May and hope this job lasts longer than my previous one (which was 10 months). Considering the current financial climate I may have jumped from the frying pan into the fire. I'm referencing October 19th and 20th, of course. "We here in the market" (ahem!) refer to it as "Black Monday," or "Melt-Down Monday"...

Actually, I work for JCB Asset Management, which is a subsidiary of J. C. Bradford. We have $125MM in managed assets (rich people bring us their money and expect us to make them richer), which is small potatoes compared to the likes of Merrill Lynch or E. F. Hutton, but it sure impressed the hell out of me. (But then what do I know). Anyway, I like my job and am learning a lot. There are eight of us in this office and I am the newest (also the most expendable).

Now comes the hard part – some of you know this already. I'm a (*whisper the next word*) grandma. I **SAID** "whisper!". Twice, yet. Tom and Josie's baby, Samantha Jo, was born last January 7th and is a little doll (naturally) and has the sweetest disposition in the world. But then, so did her father. It looks as though they will be moving back to Michigan very soon. Josie's mom has purchased a house which they are going to rent from her. Josie has been quite isolated down here and I know she will appreciate having her mom, sister, and friends around once more. But I do hate to see them leave.

John and Kim and Baby Jeremy Michael Riley Sullivan are "back on the road again" and will be home on the 20th. Jeremy was born November 4th. He was about 2-1/2 weeks early and weighed 5 lbs. 3 oz., five pounds of which was black hair! He looked just like John when he was a newborn – except John weighed 2 lbs. more. Looking at this little one it's hard to imagine two more pounds on such a tiny little body!

My folks are doing okay considering they are 76 years old – which considering, I can't. Do you realize how old that makes me? Never mind, don't answer that. My dad rented office space in town (Big Sandy) and took in some tax returns earlier this year and my mom has been writing poetry and having it published in the Camden paper so they're keeping up pretty good, I'd say. We manage some good visits back and forth every few weeks.

Caryn flew down for a visit right before Thanksgiving and stayed through that weekend. She looked beautiful, of course, and seems happy and well-adjusted and enjoying her first semi-serious romantic relationship and her sales assistant job at Prescott, Ball & Turpin (also a stock brokerage firm). She and Lisa have been sharing an apartment for several months so I think she's gotten a taste of the "real world". Lisa has a new boyfriend and spends more time with him than at the apartment. Caryn, to no avail, is hard pressed to keep tabs on her and isn't too thrilled with the "mother" role she feels has somehow befallen her. She calls about once a week to bring me up to date on the latest episodes and I am torn between amusement on one hand and sympathy and concern on the other.

On this subject, I could write a book (so could we all, I guess) and this is not the time or place. Suffice it to say, all the kids are healthy, relatively sane, and managing to cope and sometimes enjoy their lives. I have to be thankful for that.

Financially, this has been a better year than last and I am making slow but steady progress towards eliminating some debts I incurred as a result of losing two jobs and being only temporarily employed during '85 and '86. I have a **GEM** of a car – paid for except for the inevitable repairs that come with owning an antique. But it beats monthly car payments any day. It's a 1967 Buick Skylark, red body, white top. It really needs a paint job but I'm hoping to get that done this spring. THEN, I plan to show it at the Music City Chapter Buick Club of America Car Show (545 Buick owners have been invited to participate) which the Nashville chapter is hosting in April of next year (Scott and I are members). Even needing a paint job, I get stopped and asked about my car a lot. (I love it!). Eat your hearts out, guys!

Scott and I are still bumming around together, riding his motorcycle when the weather permits, and generally having as much fun as our limited time and money allow. We are also members of the local Harley-Davidson Motorcycle Club. Speaking of which, the Club made their Second Annual Fall Weekend Ride to Cherokee, North Carolina, in mid-October. Naturally we went. Except for my totally Num Bum we encountered no difficulties on the 600-mile (weekend) round trip. And the colors were gorgeous!)

Personally speaking, I am more skeptical and liberal than when I was younger (a former "close"[6] associate would probably say its because of the crowd I run with but I tend to think it's just the fruition of me).

That's about it – an encapsulated year in the life of Sarah Sullivan. I sure hope to hear from more of you this year than last and that when I do you'll fill me in on all the things you and your families have been doing. You know, don't you, that people write the kind of letters they want to receive (hint, hint).

My concept of God gets more global the older I get, and my prayer and wish for the world is that all people could experience the blessings my family and I have shared. That includes all of you, of course.

Much love and best wishes for the new year.

Sarah

> P.S. Two pages? Well, when I write only once a year, what do you expect!

---

[6] my ex – ultra-conservative – husband

**Journal Entry
September 1988**

Scott and I reached a point about two years into our relationship when we decided it might be wise to spend one weekend a month apart. To see what would happen. We would be free to see whoever we wanted and do whatever we wanted. Part of being best friends. We just would never lie about it and would always tell each other what we had done. It wasn't particularly easy for either of us but we held to our commitment of openness and honesty even so. On our weekends "off," I knew I tossed and turned restlessly all night imagining the details of who and what he was doing.

One weekend I spent Friday night with a man and stayed till around noon the next day (we had a very late breakfast). I drove to Scott's afterwards and was surprised to learn he'd driven around this man's house several times the night before in an agony of jealousy and pain. I think it surprised him, too. He did not expect to react this way.

Part of our agreement was that in telling the other person about what we did, the other person had to promise to tell the truth about how he felt about what we did. Scott made me see how important this was. At first, I felt the need to cover up my feelings. But Scott made me realize that being truthful about feelings was just as important as being truthful about actions.

I may want to do something but if I know it will hurt you very much, I may decide my desire to do it is less than my desire NOT to hurt you. In an open relationship you must be truthful with each other about your activities and feelings. The choice of what to do – or not do – is left up to each individual, however. If you can say to the other person, I love you and want to be your best friend – no matter what – and you must do what you have to do – no matter what. I know I may sometimes be hurt, but I will always tell you how I feel. If it hurts too much and seriously threatens our relationship, I will tell you that, too. I may agree in principal that freedom and openness is the best way to achieve a good, long-lasting relationship, but I may find I can't handle it.

It seemed to us both that having the freedom to act and be what we wanted to act and be was the only way our relationship could survive. If either of us put a condition on the other's behavior – it might provide temporary security, but in the long run, it would be the undoing of the relationship.

I don't want you to love me, to stay with me because I ask or require it of you. I want you to love me, to stay with me because it's what you choose to do. And the only way you can choose to love me, to stay with me is if you have the freedom to choose not to.

If you really love some thing or some body, you have to be willing to let it/them go. If you keep it or them through force or coercion or rules, you don't really have anything at all.

A lot of people would not agree or understand what I'm talking about. It isn't easy to do even if you understand it. Scott and I talked a lot about these kinds of things in the first three years of our relationship. Eventually, we came to agree that it was too difficult to have that much freedom. It caused us both too much pain. For me, I always told Scott, the hard part wasn't thinking that he had sex with another woman. It was what came after. The close warm feelings, the tenderness, the talking. That seemed so much more intimate – and therefore threatening – to me.

There's a usual goal for sex – it's called orgasm. Any two people can do it. Even alone you can do it. Sex is NOT love. But love often grows out of the close, warm feelings, the tenderness, the talking that comes after. And that's threatening.

We still have the understanding that each of us is free to do whatever we need to do. Practically speaking, however, knowing that we have that freedom makes it unnecessary to pursue that freedom. At least so far.

* * * * *

Scott's and my story began on New Years Eve, December 31, 1985, at a Parents Without Partners function. We had met a couple of weeks earlier at a PWP Sunday Pot Luck Dinner. I had noticed this beautiful Harley Davidson motorcycle parked outside the apartment where the dinner was held.

The first thing I wanted to know after greeting everyone was "who belongs to the motorcycle". It was Scott. I think he was surprised at my interest and past involvement with this machine. I didn't look the type. But then neither did he. We exchanged the usual getting to know you questions adding information about our bike interest and experiences.

I had gone to the New Years Party with Mark. We were good friends more than lovers, and felt free to circulate at will.

Scott asked me to dance. As we danced, I realized he was shorter than any man I had ever dated. But attractive. That evening was the first and last time I seriously noticed his height, however. As I got to know him, his integrity and values made him seem ten feet tall in my estimation.

He called me the next Wednesday and we made dinner plans for the following Saturday. But since he was coming down in the late afternoon to visit his dad who lived a couple of miles from me, I suggested fixing steak, salad, and baked potatoes at my apartment. He brought the steaks.

After dinner we took a drive in his car out in the country surrounding Franklin. Since cows and barns and trees and grass are my most favorite smells in the world, it was delightful to learn he loved the country just as much as I did.

It was also delightful to learn he was a talker, since my ex-husband was not. I had found Scott physically attractive when we met and this first date was showing him to be thoughtful, intelligent, and respectful and admiring of women as a gender. Although I didn't completely realize it that first date, he was, in fact, a feminist. And I had known few males I could thus classify.

We eventually returned to my apartment to finish off the evening as you might expect any two grown up single adults to do. Brazen hussy that I was, I invited him to my bed. He spent the night. And most of the next day. He had a car club meeting the next afternoon but returned and we spent another passionate evening talking and loving and generally being consumed by each other. I think it's called Falling In Love.

Falling In Love is the exhilarating, passionate experience common to so many. But it's what happens when you start to come down, or normalize your feelings, that determine whether a relationship has a future. The more Scott and I learned about each other, the closer we became.

Our feelings were strong and our intellects seemed to validate this was not simply a whirlwind fling. But for different reasons, each of us was cautious about making a commitment. I know my cautiousness was because I didn't want to spoil a good thing – a great thing, actually. If something is working, and working well, why take the chance of changing it.

I was so overwhelmed by the "fit" of this relationship. Up until 1984 I had, after all, led a pretty sheltered life. I had known two men in my life. With each of them, once we passed the Falling In Love stage, the relationships slowly began to deteriorate. I had desperately wanted and needed a best friend – but nothing in my limited experience led me to believe a lover and best friend could be one and the same.

As we came to know each other better, Scott, my lover, was becoming my Best Friend. And I was learning to be his.

Being a best friend to someone you love and have an on-going relationship with is not an easy thing to do. Scott and I talked a great deal about what a best friend is – or isn't.

If I am your best friend, I want what's best for you. What if you tell me you want to go out with another person? If I love you, I am probably threatened by this. But would I rather have you not go out and secretly wish you had? Or go out and lie about it? Maybe none of these choices are designed to make me happy, but the first is by far the least destructive to our relationship. A best friend can easily say, "If this is something you want, go for it." A best friend who is also a lover, has to be very secure in himself to deal with this situation. But it can be dealt with. I did it for Scott. And he did it for me.

We talked a lot about the differences in men and women. Without blame. This did not seem difficult for us to do, though, I think women, especially, often have a hard time dealing with the sexual nature of men.

I had been in a restrictive, demeaning, unfulfilling relationship for 22 years. I was ready to do some exploring, some experimenting. I was 46 years old, my life was galloping by. I had been responsible and sensible and serious all my life. And look where it had got me. It was time for some fun and excitement before it was too late.

Scott seemed to personify the free spirit I wanted to be. He was always ready to go anywhere, do anything. He loved cars and had one he raced. He owned a Harley and took 2-3 day trips on it several times each year. He loved to visit new places and didn't have a time-frame for reaching his destination. He thought the "getting there" of the journey was just as important – maybe more so – than the destination. He loved driving his bike or car on the "back roads". And if a "Y" in the road, or an old barn or country store showed up somewhere along the way, it was usually worth checking out.

Laid back, adventuresome, spontaneous. He helped me rediscover these things in myself. He was a kindred spirit, my alter-ego. We joined the Nashville chapter of the Harley-Davidson Motorcycle Club and I began attending the Buick Club of America meetings with him. We raced around the country on his bike or in his car from one excursion after another. Till financial difficulties made it necessary for him to sell the bike.

How I miss those rides. Especially the ones we took on summer evenings right after coming home from work. We'd just grab our helmets and jackets, jump on the bike, and away we'd go. Out into the country. Stopping somewhere along the way at a roadside café for a burger and a coke. It would be dark when we returned, of course, and usually we'd finish the ride by making a pass through downtown Nashville (which was only 4 miles away from where we lived) for a glimpse of the night-time activity. We learned to recognize certain individuals, street people, actually, who had their own special haunts for dealing with life on the street.

We dropped out of the motorcycle club once he sold the bike, of course. But we sure enjoyed the trips we took with them for a couple of years. One was to the Buffalo River (about 75 miles from Nashville) for a day of canoeing. Saturday day trips of this nature were common. The best trip, however, was in mid-October when they drove to Cherokee, North Carolina. It was their big activity for Fall and they picked the weekend when the leaf color was expected to be at its peak. We left early Saturday morning and returned late Sunday night. 600 miles round trip in two days on the back seat of a motorcycle is the true test for a biker bitch, believe me. I had a numb bum for two days afterwards! But I wouldn't have missed it for the world.

We talked a great deal about relationships. Being a bachelor for 12 years, Scott had lots of experiences with relationships. We both felt this relationship was "special", but neither of us expected it to last. We just wanted to enjoy it as much as we could for as long as we could. (We're still doing just that.)

We both agreed that trust – the consequence of honesty – is the most important ingredient. Actually, you can't have a relationship without it. Too many times, we hold back or distort the truth to save ourselves or our partners when, in fact, deception is the one thing guaranteed to destroy any relationship. Telling me the truth may hurt but the alternative is beyond bearable. At least that's what we believed and tried to practice in the early years of our relationship.

And it was good.

— He Shines —

He shines . . .

He's at the gate
inside his b-b-b-bad Buick
on the drag strip.
Muscles tense, adrenalin high
he "revs" up the engine and does a "burn-out"
to get the tires hot and wet for a good bite
when the light turns green.

The top light flashes
and then he counts the seconds
five and . . .
four and . . .
three and . . .
Two and . . .
GO!

The car shoots forward
almost seeming to leave the pavement
for an instant
but the torque is strong
and the nose stays down.
He's half a car length ahead at the start
now a full length
and more
and more.

He finishes the quarter mile
four car lengths ahead of his competition
Time . . . . 12.8 seconds!
Oh, yes
that's one b-b-b-bad Buick
and one b-b-b-bad dude.

He jumps from the car
I run to give and get a great big hug
he's grinning from ear to ear . . .
He Shines.

He shines . . .
He talks about his beliefs
his philosophy of life
which comes from somewhere deep inside
and has nothing to do
with doctrines or shoulds and should nots
as set down by organized religion
He says he's not religious –
but he is
in the truest sense of the word.
His integrity and honesty seem to me
to be above the goals and aspirations
of most "good" people.

His choice are not made
out of fear of retribution
or hope of reward.
In a world of changing values
his goodness is constant
not based on exterior controls and forces
but coming from a "still small voice" inside . . .
He Shines.

He shines . . .

He's raised above me
the room is nearly dark
but the flickering candle
casts a sensuous glow about the room.
His eyes are closed
his arms extended
to support his body above me
which is moving in rhythmic movements
up and down.

His thrusts are strong and steady
each time pulling nearly out
causing that beautiful throbbing muscle
to touch and stimulate me
in all the right places.

Each time he pushes back into my hot, wet center
I feel a burst of delight and pleasure
which intensifies
as I gaze up to see
the look of concentration and pleasure
that is written on his face.

Thrusting stronger
the muscle expands
bigger and harder
our pleasure peaks.
Oh, yes . . .

He Shines

Sure Was Fun While it Lasted

*Nashville Harley Hog Club,
Trip to Smokey Mountains,
Fall 1986*

December 15, 1988

Merry Christmas from Nashville,

Ah d'clare, seems lak I jist don't know wher the tahm goes. Seems lak I jist got these here doo-dads put away frum las Chrismus and now I got to git 'em out agin.

Well, now that you know who this is from . . . hope it finds you healthy and happy.

To bring you up to date – which is what you want . . . right?

John and Kim and Jeremy (who turned one in November and is Beautiful and Brilliant) keep busy traveling the highways and byways on the Jessie Special (bus, that is). They're heading into their slow season now and won't be too busy with shows till after the first of the year.

Tom and Josie are settled down in Warren, Michigan, and produced their second baby (my third grandchild), a girl, Carrie Michelle, last May 31st. Samantha (Sammy Jo) will be two in January. Grandma thinks they're both Beautiful and Brilliant, too.

Caryn keeps busy between her job at Hertz Rent-A-Car and her boyfriend, Ed. She has her own apartment in Royal Oak and enjoys her independence. She has an aptitude for and interest in accounting and says she wants to get started back to school "one of these days" to pursue a business degree with an accounting major. Now, if she'll just put her want with her will – and not wait too long doing it.

Pie (Lisa, that is) – my baby – got married a few months ago and she and her husband are expecting a baby sometime in March or April. She thinks March, the doctor says April. Originally, he told her March 21st (you know what that means, of course. Another chance for 3 generations of St. Paddy's babies. Caryn was supposed to be the third, of course, but that's the first time she waited too long!) [7]

---

[7] I was born on my mother's birthday, March 17th. My third child and first girl, Caryn, was due March 19th. She arrived on the 20th!

SARAH'S STORY

My best friend and alter-ego, Scott, is about to begin a new career. After weighing the pros and cons a long time, all the pros seemed to fall in (to place) and the cons fell out. He's just signed on with Builders Transport as a truck driver after completing eight weeks of school in Bowling Green, Kentucky, (commuting every day!). This week he's in Memphis taking another class for Builder's – PSP 101 (Paper Shuffling Process 101). He'll be home Thursday and they told him to have a nice weekend because he and his trainer will be on the road for the next several weeks. He does get back for Christmas, and then the runs are 14-20 days with 3-4 days at home between trips. After eight more weeks of driving with his trainer, he'll be on his own.

He's had a love affair with motors since he was about fifteen – whether it's fixing them, driving them, or (the most fun) racing them, and has always been fascinated by trucks, plus he loves to travel – so he decided to "follow his bliss(*). With the changes and upgrading going on in the trucking industry, he thinks there will be some good opportunities to grow with the industry after he's had a couple of years over-the-road experience. They desperately need teachers (trainers) and qualified, experienced people. So we feel optimistic.

So now . . . **I WANT TO DRIVE A TRUCK, TOO**. First it was motorcycles, now trucks? (I don't have to explain or justify. I'm in my second childhood. I'm entitled.). Actually, I'd settle for riding along on some of his trips, which may be possible sometime. As soon as I come up with a good "handle", I can fill the airways over the byways of America with my own special brand of nonsense (with which you're all so familiar).

To continue . . . I managed to get to Michigan once this summer. Lisa came down on the bus with Jessie and troupe surprising me a few days before I was scheduled to go there so we flew back together. They have a nice apartment in Sterling Heights and she keeps it "neat as a pin" (takes after her mom, of course).

Caryn flew down unexpectedly in early November because she got a wedding invitation from her best girlfriend from her Tennessee high school days. She flew down on Thursday night and back on Monday morning. We had a great time even if we did get stranded in Franklin on Friday night after the wedding (in the pouring rain) and had to call Scott to come and rescue us. (I guess I'm destined to go through life getting stranded somewhere, sometime, in some car). We even managed a nice visit with my folks on Saturday. Speaking of whom, they are doing quite well for youngsters of 76 years who are in the process of selling their home in Big Sandy and moving back to Jackson – to their **fourth** final home (positively, absolutely . . . says my dad).

Lisa and her husband, Mo, surprised me by paying for me to fly to Michigan for Thanksgiving. What a treat! John and Kim were there, too, so we all (the kids and me) were together for that holiday for the first time in several years. It was **WONDERFUL**. I got there Wednesday evening so we planned our dinner for Friday. Lisa and I did the shopping and preparation on Thursday. I was SO proud of her – she is SO organized (like me – did I say that already?). I had brought my silver candlesticks, a centerpiece, and a fancy tablecloth. Well, I didn't know what she did or didn't have and it WAS Thanksgiving, after all. She had everything else we needed to set a pretty holiday table. There were 12 of us and we had a great time. I even managed **NOT** to burn the rolls!

Early (7 a.m.) the next Sunday morning Tom rented a car and drove Kim, John and Jeremy to South Bend, Indiana, for Jessie's shows at 2 and 6 p.m. that day. Lisa, Mo, and I rented another car and drove down later. We got there just in time for the 6 p.m. show. We all went out to eat together afterwards, as usual, and that's when Jessie and Mickey got to meet Lisa's new husband.

He is twelve years older than Lisa, comes from Jordan, and will charm his way into your heart five minutes after you met him. At least that's the effect he's had on Caryn, me, Kim, Jessie – and Lisa, of course. In his culture, women, children, and families are cherished, protected, and honored in many ways that we here in America seem to have forgot. Liberation has its points – but so does chivalry. So what we have here is a marriage that will, hopefully, be a blend of both worlds.

Moving on . . .

John and Kim will be in Michigan for the traditional Sullivan family Christmas. My memories of those special family times are so poignant at this time of year. With Tom and Josie living back in Michigan now, it means all the kids, and their kids, can be together with their dad and his family. Even though I miss them, I'm happy knowing they can have that special time together. John and Kim do have to rush back on the 26th, of course for the Riley tradition of Christmas in Texas with Kim's grandparents.

Lisa and Mo may come down for the holidays. Scott and I will drive down to Franklin for Christmas breakfast with his family. As usual, I will plan dinner for whichever day is best for my folks and whoever else can get here. My brother, his girlfriend, Kathy, and her daughter may come down from Michigan. Christmas in Tennessee is a little quieter perhaps, but it's still a time for counting the blessings of family, friends . . . and alter-egos.

Well, I tried to use wide margins and small type so I could squeeze everything into one page but of course I didn't make it.

It's a shame we are losing track of each other except for once a year or so. As usual I should apologize for this epistle but since I would be *DELIGHTED* to get a two-page letter from each of you I hope you will indulge me.

May we all enjoy health and contentment in this coming year. And may we use at least some of our wisdom and energies to promote a world in which everything in it – people, plants, and animals – is valued as a "thou", rather than an "it".(**).

Love, Sarah

(*) A phrase coined by Joseph Campbell--from a six-hour special nterview with Bill Moyers, aired last fall on PBS.

(**) The Power of Thou, From Joseph Campbell's <u>The Power of Myth</u>, pp. 78- 79; "The Indians addressed all of life as a 'thou' – the trees, the stones, everything. You can address anything as a 'thou,' and if you do it, you can feel the change in your own psychology. The ego that sees a 'thou' is not the same ego that sees an 'it'. And when you go to war with people, the problem of the newspapers is to turn those people into 'its.'

SARAH'S STORY

December 15, 1989

Dear Friends,

I just can't seem to give up this Dawn-habit (*) of writing Christmas letters. Even though it's been ages since I've seen most of you – and a year since I've written.

I would love to see each one of you. Let's plan a party. We'll all meet somewhere in the middle of the country . . . say, Louisville, Kentucky. Well, it is **kind of** in the middle – I can't help it if it's closer for me than you.

I have some vacation time coming during the week between Christmas and New Year's and Scott and I had planned to drive up to Michigan in my newly "restored" 67 Buick Skylark. (When it rained . . . it really rained – inside my car, that is. So in the process of fixing the leaks and making sure it **never** leaks again, I had it repainted – new white vinyl top, bright red body – as original). We hoped to make a stop near Chicago (spelled B-a-r-r-i-n-g-t-o-n)[8] on the way up or down. Scott started a new job a few weeks ago and is now driving for Schneider National Trucking Company so vacation time for him is out.

So then I thought I could drive up with Anne (my other best friend) or come by myself. But when I saw how far Chicago was from the beaten path to Michigan I had to nix that portion of the trip.

So then my folks called to say they finally sold their house. Closing is December 21st and the new owners want to move in as soon as possible. So – it looks like I'd better get my butt over there and help them pack. Nix Michigan altogether.

They're finally moving into that "fourth final house" I mentioned in last year's letter but how they'll manage, I don't know. I've got to do what I can to help. Mom fell and broke her back last March.

---

[8] Best Bud, Wayne, from High School

Actually, she crushed several vertebrae and will probably never fully recover. Considering she could have been killed or paralyzed, however, her recovery is amazing. She was going down the steps to the lake to fish, they were rotten (the steps, not the fish) and broke when she stepped on them. She did a somersault and landed down on the beach twelve feet below!

The children and grandchildren are fine. Tom and Josie have just moved into their very own first home. John drove up this past weekend to help them. John and Kim still haven't sold their mobile home so John keeps busy with extra jobs when they're in town. (They have been in **their** first home for nearly a year). Jeremy just turned two and talks more every time I see him . . . He's absolutely wonderful.

Sammy Jo, Carrie, and Leila were absolutely wonderful the last time I saw them – which was a few months ago. Wonder if they've changed? . . . Naaah. Sammy has the most beautiful big blue eyes and such a loving disposition. Carrie was just beginning to take off with her walking plus sticking her fingers into whatever opening she could find . . . like your eyes, your nose.

Leila was four months old when I last saw her and a total delight. Dark black hair . . . blue, blue eyes . . . pierced (pierced?) ears?! Lisa had it done while I was there. I mean literally while I was with her! I couldn't stand it! She said they were tired of people coming up to say, "What a beautiful little boy!" Lisa is going to school part-time taking Accounting. YAY!!! Why did I learn too late that MATH is POWER and POWER is MONEY . . . (or is it the other way around???)

Caryn moved back to Tennessee last June. She stayed with me for a few months practicing up on her "Southern". In November she moved into a house with two other girls . . . **both** of whom are going to school and working. One is a full-time student at Vanderbilt. Let's hope some of that latent ambition and drive will ignite in Caryn.

SARAH'S STORY

In between Scott's trips home, Anne and I keep busy with visits to the Spa (we have now managed to close TWO of them; don't ask me how!), lectures and programs at Vanderbilt and/or church, or just trying to keep up with all the great programs on Channel 8 (our public television station). Plus I joined the church bowling league. Luckily I go just for fun! Anne is self-employed (formerly an auditor and then a securities broker for Merrill Lynch) but says she's about ready to fulfill her real ambition and become a "bag lady". She owns **THREE** VCR's – so she can watch and record one program while she's taping a tape! And you thought I was crazy. Actually, she's a delight and a wonderful friend.

It's really great to have two best buddies. I hope you all have two – or more – and that you have some wonderfully happy times with them in 1990. Just maybe Scott and I can stop by your house in my classy red Skylark for a visit sometime this coming year. That would still be alright, wouldn't it?

Love, Sarah

P.S. The kerosene in the lamp is still lit.

(*) Had to use my real name here since "Sarah-habit" removes the play on words.

I don't know what happened to my Christmas 1990 letter. But this letter written to Wayne and Cora Lee in February of that year pretty well expresses who and where I was at that time.

* * * * *

February 2, 1990

Dear Wayne and Cora Lee,

It was great to hear from you at Christmas! Thanks so much – you don't know how much I appreciate it. The only cards I got from "the old gang" were from you, Ruth, and Nan and Tom Smith.

And I loved the picture. Cora Lee – you look great! Wayne, you looked so good I just wanted to hug you! And the boys are gorgeous.

Every year I think I won't write any more Christmas chronologies – so much time has passed since I've seen or even talked with the people on my list. But somehow, I can't stop doing it. The holidays are memory days, and my thoughts often turn to old times and old friends. That letter has become my only contact – and I just can't let go of it. Since I still love hearing from all **my** old buddies, I just keep on, hoping they'll do the same. You do – and it means a lot.

I was saddened to hear of your mom's passing, Cora Lee. There is no pain like losing a parent or child, I'm certain. Fortunately, I haven't had to face either yet but that time is coming ever closer (with my folks, that is; I hope I never have to face the other).

My dad has been frail for a number of years (barely weighs 100 pounds); I'm surprised he has any lungs left. And since her fall, my mom has not been the same, mentally or physically. She had to take a lot of medicine in connection with her injury plus the regular medications she's been on for years – for angina and high blood pressure and some other stuff, I think. She recently got down to 105 pounds herself so my dad took her to the doctor. Her blood pressure was dangerously low – 80 over 50, I think he said. The

SARAH'S STORY

doctor also said she was "over-medicated" and took her off **all** the medicine. (This in spite of the fact that her previous doctor had said she should never go off the angina medicine; according to him it could precipitate a heart attack – I guess you just have to trust whoever your current physician is and hope for the best). He did give her an anti-depressant, however. I know she's been very depressed since the accident. But then, who wouldn't be? She is very forgetful now (maybe from the medicine and I wonder if it's reversible).

I hope your dad continues to be okay, Wayne.

I do wish we could visit sometime. If Scott and I could ever get a long weekend I would love to drive up and see you. I would love for my best friend to meet some of my favorite people. When I say "best friend", I really mean just that – think of all the ways a person is who is your best friend – and that's Scott.

I guess my old buddies that I haven't seen for so long would think I've changed a lot from the olden days. But then, you've probably changed, too. Having been with myself the whole time, however, I think I've just evolved to this place that I am mostly from circumstances and reading and thinking. Also, I've met some really neat people along the way – most of whom I'd never have known in my "other" life. Some rich, some poor; some really smart, some just regular. And all of them have enriched my life in one way or another. (For instance, our basement apartment is presently rented by a young man named David; he's 25 and Gay. He's one of 11 children (the rest are girls) and grew up in the country around the Grand Canyon with a succession of alcoholic step-fathers. His mother is a real "pioneer woman" – doesn't use electricity, builds (literally, herself) her own houses, septic tanks, etc. Scott and Anne and I are going to take a trip out there to meet her! David's had a rough life in many ways and yet there is beauty is some of it, too. At one time his mom had a 10-acre flower garden!

He's going through a tough time financially and socially right now having just moved here from Ohio; I've kind of adopted him).

Since becoming a working woman (without a degree) myself, I have come to identify more strongly with the "have-nots" than the "haves" anyway. How on earth I ended up working at a stock brokerage firm is one of life's little ironies. Talk about conservative! Jerry would feel right at home, of course. I, of course, keep my opinions to myself – yes, I do – really. (It's called knowing where the butter comes from – or something like that).

My office has seven people of which I am the least educated and paid. But politics and economics notwithstanding, they are the most professional people with whom I have ever worked. Their bread and butter comes from developing skills of thoughtfulness, respect, and consideration, and it carries over into everything they do. There is one other clerical person besides myself in the group. Our boss, Paul, gave each of us a Christmas card – with a $100 bill in it! We both cried – **not** in front of him.

Incidentally, he came to head our office last May from Chicago, having worked at Stein Roe & Farnham for 18 years – his name is Paul Kuhn. He is wonderful to work for and extremely good at what he does. (In case you might have heard of SR or PK).

To continue . . . Most of the time I don't like the "status quo". I think we are running out of time to make changes for the better, particularly with regard to the safety and well-being of this beloved and only earth home. I have come to **L-O-V-E** the "L" word – as defined in the dictionary. (Can you believe it, Wayne, I voted for Dukkakis! – Now please don't tell me you've changed, too – and become a Republican – and voted for Bush!!! . . . You have, I just **know** it!).[9]

I've been attending the Unitarian church for several years. No preaching, thanks. (Whatever you've heard, forget it. If you want to **know** who and what they are – go check it out yourself.)

---

(9) Wayne and I were Best Buds in high school; my folks were staunch Republicans, his parents were 'dyed-in-the-wool' Democrats. Now, it seems, the tables were reversed.

I hate guns, I think there is a place for pornography. But I still think the smell of the country – cows and hay and manure – is the best smell in the world and falling down barns with snow on the roof make the loveliest paintings. I'm content to be who I am, where I am, although I wouldn't turn down a few extra million brain cells if I could get them.

And I still pour my heart out in letters! I guess if my life depended on it I could write a one or two paragraph letter, but I'm not sure. Why I always feel the need to tell "who" I am – and why – I really don't know. But I do, don't I. I would love to spend a weekend sharing what the last ten years have wrought us.

I'm through now.

Do you keep in touch with Julie and Jim? I haven't heard from them in two years and am concerned. The cards I sent last year and this didn't come back so I assume they haven't moved – but I just don't know. My cards to Connie and Terry and Jenny and Steve Innes were returned. I've written Jerry asking if he has their current addresses.

I must stop. It's after 7 p.m. I can't believe this letter! It was just going to be a "get back in touch" kind of thing . . .

It's all your fault, Wayne. You did say, "Please write."

Love, Sarah

WEDDING SERVICE AND DINNER
Sunday, June 30, 1991

Sarah Sullivan and Scott Jensen

5:15 p.m.
MUSIC WHILE GUESTS ARE BEING SEATED
"Dream Lady," Tom Scott
"When A Man Loves A Woman," Wes Montgomery
"You Are So Beautiful To Me," Bob James

5:30 p.m.
MUSIC AFTER GUESTS ARE SEATED
"That's All I Need To Know," by Linda Ronstadt, Aaron Neville

DAVID MAYNARD
Personal Comments about Scott
"Whiter Shade of Pale," by Bill Black
Personal Comments about Sarah
"She," by Zamfir

Sarah Sullivan
Personal Comments about Scott
"He Shines," by Sheena Easton

Scott Jensen
Personal Comments about Sarah
"My Woman, My Lover, My Friend," by Jackie Wilson

WEDDING SERVICE AND EXCHANGE OF VOWS
"Daisy A Day, " by Jud Strunk

6:30 P.M.
DINNER

INTRODUCTORY COMMENTS BY DAVID MAYNARD

Scott and Sarah have asked me to welcome you. They are happy to have you share in their wedding celebration and dinner.

Before exchanging their marriage vows, they want to take a few minutes to share with you their reasons for being here today by way of personal comments and music which are meaningful to them and which they hope you will enjoy.

They have asked me to share with you some observations about who and what they were just prior to their meeting.

As 1985 drew to a close, Scott was approaching mid-life pretty much the same way he had spent most of his life. His life-style could be described as that of a "free spirit". His life had been in constant flux – friends, family, jobs and residences had come and gone. He moved frequently, making friendships easily but always moving on – to start again. Permanence in family and personal relationships and jobs had somehow managed to elude him. But he had a passion for "hot" race cars and Harley-Davidson motorcycles and loved the feeling of freedom he got from riding and taking trips at a moment's notice. New people, places, and friends were exciting. Still, something was missing.

Like most of us he had a private dream that included a special companion who would share his interests and beliefs. His friendships with women had all been temporary. He was never satisfied. Always, these relationships came to an end. That was just a way of life – his life, anyway. "Happily ever after" was the stuff of fairy tales. Real life just wasn't that way.

PLAY "WHITER SHADE OF PALE" by Bill Black.

About this same time Sarah was embarking on the "passage" in her life that women face as they approach their middle years. Having spent most of her adult life being a wife and mother, she was now divorced, the children were grown – or nearly so – and she was about to enter a period of time that would provide her with the opportunity to rediscover who she was. With no responsibility to anyone but herself, she was experiencing a new sense of self and freedom.

Family responsibilities were over. A new chapter in her life was beginning. Although she didn't think it likely at her age, tucked deep within her heart was the dream that somewhere "out there" was a man who could be her best friend. More than anything else, she had always wanted a companion that was a best friend.

PLAY "SHE" by Zamfir
COMMENTS BY Sarah

I know I was drawn to Scott partly because of the freedom he seemed to represent. He was carefree and full of the joy of life. He was just so much fun to be with! Yet he was thoughtful and caring and had a high regard for women. It didn't hurt, of course, that I found him attractive, too. As we explored each other's feelings and points of view, a feeling of kinship developed.

As a young girl I had delighted in the Lucy Montgomery books about Anne of Green Gables. Anne identified people by whether or not they were "kindred spirits". Scott was definitely a kindred spirit. He has acted like a best friend from the first day we met. One important reason is because from the very beginning we have treated each other with respect. And we have been totally honest in our dealings with one another.

Another thing Scott has done for me – and it may be the most special thing of all – he has provided a place – a very safe place – for me to be me. He likes me, he really likes me. He accepts me so unconditionally that I am free to be or say or do whatever it is I need to say or be or do. And he's right there next to me saying, "Go for it, honey".

Another reason why we're here today is because we communicate. And that means talk. We have talked, and talked . . . and talked. Sometimes even more than either of us want to right then, we have talked. But we were talkers before we met. We believe in talking – in communicating – because it works. We've never yelled at each other – or spoken cruel words. And never separated with one of us being hurt or confused. Even the best of friends can misunderstand each other sometimes. Talking through to the point of understanding takes time and effort – but the results are always worth it.

When Scott and I first started seeing each other, I heard a song that seemed to exactly express the way I felt about him. I guess it had been popular for a couple of years but I heard it for the first time a few months after meeting him. It had such an impact on me that I wrote a poem for him based on the song. The poem has three verses and I would like to read one of them now. It is the verse that talks about the kind of person I believe him to be.

After I read one verse of my poem entitled, "He Shines", we will play the song of the same name by Sheena Easton.

> He shines . . .
> He talks about his beliefs
> His philosophy of life
> Which comes from somewhere deep inside
> And has nothing to do
> With doctrines – or "shoulds" and "should nots"
> As set down by organized religion.
> He says he's not religious
> But he is
> In the truest sense of the word.
> His integrity and honesty seem to me
> To be above the goals and aspirations
> Of most "good" people.
> His choices are not made
> Out of fear of retribution
> Or hope of reward.
> In a world of changing values
> His goodness is constant
> Not being based on exterior controls and forces
> But from a "still small voice" inside . . .
> He shines.

SARAH'S STORY

PLAY "HE SHINES" by Sheena Easton.
COMMENTS BY Scott

It has been my experience that there aren't too many exceptional people in this world – at least not in mine. When you think about it though, I guess if there were we wouldn't consider them exceptional. Anyway, I didn't have to know Sarah very long to begin thinking she was exceptional. At least in ways that are important to me. She is even tempered . . . and kind . . . and considerate . . . and reasonable.

I don't trust people with unpredictable temperaments. And Sarah is definitely predictable, maybe I should say "dependable". That doesn't mean she isn't spontaneous at times – especially when it comes to having fun, that is. But it's the ways in which she's predictable and even tempered that mean so much to me.

She is assertive without being mean. She is nurturing without being patronizing. She gives love and kindness without keeping score. And she can be reverent without being dogmatic. Predictable and reasonable – that's what she is. In my book, that makes her exceptional. And that's why she's my best friend – and in about five more minutes, she's going to be my wife!

PLAY "MY WOMAN, MY LOVER, MY FRIEND"
by Jackie Wilson.
WEDDING SERVICE (David Maynard)

Dear Friends, we are gathered here at this hour to witness and to celebrate the drawing together of two separate lives. We have come so that this man, Scott, and this woman, Sarah, may be joined in marriage. It is not to be entered into lightly but with certainty, with mutual respect, and with a sense of reverence which does not preclude beauty, humor, or joy.

Love can be one of the highest experiences that comes to humankind. At its best it reduces our selfishness, deepens our personalities, and makes life far more meaningful.

All significant experiences are of concern to our fellow men and women. Two people in love do not live in isolation from the wider embraces of humanity. To achieve love is not to be absolved of social responsibility. So it is that the institution of marriage is ordained as a public recognition of the private experience of love and as a sanctifying of both parties to its greatest purposes.

Matrimony symbolizes the ultimate intimacy between a man and a woman; yet this closeness should not diminish but strengthen the individuality of each partner. A marriage that lasts is one that always has a little more to grow. The poet Rainer Maria Rilke once said that marriage is not a matter "of creating a quick community of spirit by tearing down and destroying all boundaries, but rather a good marriage is that in which each appoints the other guardian of his solitude . . . once the realization is accepted that even between the closest human beings infinite distances continue to exist, a wonderful living side by side can grow up, if they succeed in loving the distance between them no less than one another."

Kahlil Gibran echoed these sentiments in <u>The Prophet</u>:

"Sing and dance together and be joyous, but let
each one of you be alone.
Even as the strings of a lute are alone though
they quiver with the same music. . .
And stand together yet not too near together;
For the pillars of the temple stand apart,
And the oak tree and the cypress grow not in
each other's shadow."

Thus it is out of the resonance between individuality and union that love, whose incredible strength is equal only to its incredible fragility, is born and reborn.

Today's celebration of human affection is therefore the outward sign of a sacred and inward commitment which religious societies may consecrate and states may legalize, but which neither can create or annul. Such union can only be created by loving purpose, be maintained by abiding will, and be renewed by human feelings and intentions. In this spirit, these two persons stand before us.

Will you now please clasp your right hands?

DAVID: Do you, Scott, take Sarah to be the wife of your days, to love and to cherish, to honor and to comfort, in sorrow or in joy, in hardship or in ease, to have and to hold from this day forth?

SCOTT: I do.

DAVID: Do you, Sarah, take Scott to be the husband of your days, to love and to cherish, to honor and to comfort, in sorrow or in joy, in hardship or in ease, to have and to hold from this day forth?

SARAH: I do.

DAVID: Scott, what pledge do you offer in token of these vows?

(Ed hands ring to Scott who gives it to David)

SCOTT: This ring.

DAVID: As you place this ring, symbol of your commitment in marriage, on the third finger of Sarah's left hand, repeat after me: With this ring I wed you and pledge my faithful love.

SCOTT: With this ring I wed you and pledge my faithful love.

DAVID: Sarah, what pledge do you offer in token of these vows?

SARAH: This ring.

DAVID: As you place this ring, symbol of your commitment in marriage, on the third finger of Scott's left hand, repeat after me: With this ring I wed you and pledge my faithful love.

SARAH: With this ring I wed you and pledge my faithful love.

DAVID: Forasmuch as Scott and Sarah have consented together in wedlock, and have pledged themselves each to the other in the presence of these witnesses, I do now pronounce that they are husband and wife. Let all others honor their decision and the threshold of their house.

"For one human being to love another; that is perhaps the hardest of all our tasks" (says Rilke again), "the ultimate test and proof, the work for which all other work is but preparation . . .

Love . . . is a high inducement to the individual to ripen, to become something in himself, to become . . . a world to himself for another's sake . . . human love consists in this, that two solitudes protect and touch and greet each other."

It was not without intent that Scott and Sarah chose jazz selections as the music that greeted you as you entered this room today. A conjugal relationship may be compared to a performance of jazz, in which the crucial test for the musician is to make his mistakes mean something. May the same be true of you, Sarah and Scott, as you continually share in each other's confrontation with reality. And may you be energetic on one another's behalf, even as each of you remains ambitious for your own development.

We have witnessed this evening a humanist commitment openly acknowledged by Scott and Sarah. Marriage has always connoted not the breaking of old family ties but their transformation.

Different, more mature relationships have now to be forged anew between the grown offspring who have married and their parents. The essence of the spiritual life is how well you live, not what creeds you profess or what rituals, liturgical or social, you observe. As the great religions at their best have recognized, it is to this moral factor that we should be most loyal.

Sarah and Scott have elected to live together not according to the religious loyalties of their separate families but to mark a new path with values congenial to their own view of the world.

May these two people, now married, fulfill this covenant which they have made. May they openly give and take from each other, encouraging each other in whatever trials that may befall them, sharing in each other's joys, helping each other as each occasion requires. Having grown to trust themselves and each other, may they be unafraid to trust and welcome life. Yet may they not merely accept and give affection between themselves but also seek the lonely and the outcast in friendship. May they be willing and grateful to return love.

We who are present, and those not here who care, hope that the inspiration of this hour will not be forgotten. May they ever seek to achieve the perspective of serenity amidst conflict and of courage amidst any twilight of despair. Novelist George Eliot once asked: "What greater thing is there for two human souls than to feel that they are joined . . . to strengthen each other . . . and to be one with each other in silent unspeakable memories."

Ladies and gentlemen, may I present. . .

                Mr. and Mrs. Scott Jensen.

(Scott — KISS Sarah — YES, IN FRONT OF
ALL THESE PEOPLE — NOW!)

PLAY "DAISY A DAY" as Sarah and Scott present each guest with a daisy and a hug, starting with Sarah's parents, then Scott's dad. Guests will move to the end of the room which has been prepared for dinner.

6:30 P.M.
DINNER
Toast
Dinner, Dinner Music

7:30-8:00 P.M.
Cut wedding cake and distribute to guests.

Second Time Around . . .

The Wedding, June 1991

Cade's Cove, Wedding Trip, June 1991

And They Lived Happily Ever After . . .

SARAH'S STORY

December 20, 1991

Dear Friends,

Hope this finds you well and happy and looking forward to the new year. Each one passes ever more quickly, doesn't it.

I know you're all waiting expectantly for my yearly update so I'll get right to The News.

In May of this year I made a giant leap in the corporate ladder – moving from Secretary to Administrative Assistant – TaDa!! (Basically a lateral move – as I'm sure you realize). As a result, my boss sent me to Chicago shortly thereafter to attend a one-day seminar in Advent (a software program for securities reporting and accounting). He also gave me a bonus. So I invited Scott to go with me. Chicago is really a neat town to visit. We flew up on Thursday evening, I attended the seminar all day Friday, and then we met Wayne and Cora Lee for dinner Friday night. It was amazing to realize it had been ten years since I'd seen them. We had a delicious dinner and a great visit. It would take more than four hours to really catch up on ten years but we gave it a good try. We did some tourist things on Saturday and flew back to Nashville Saturday evening. Now, who wants to meet us after the next seminar?

Oh, by the way, Scott and I legalized our relationship by getting married last June 30th. We invited our immediate families (about 25 people) to the service and dinner which was held at a lodge called Shadowbrook about 15 miles from here. It's actually a large home that has been in this family for about 60 years and they use the downstairs for catered parties. On the outside it looks like an English Tudor castle and sits on the edge of a small lake. Inside it's very rustic with wood floors, log walls, beamed ceilings and fireplaces.

Our wedding service was rather unusual in that it lacked the "traditional" wedding music. But since we wrote it ourselves, we thought it was perfect. Our Unitarian minister talked about each of us, who and what we were when we met, and then I talked about Scott, and then Scott talked about me, and then we exchanged vows and rings, and then our minister talked again. We did play music between the speeches, however!

The minister had asked me to write everything down for the rehearsal and when I presented him with four pages of typing, he began to laugh. I asked if he was laughing because it looked so long and said, "Don't worry, it only takes about 30 minutes." He kept laughing as he said, "My usual wedding takes about five **minutes!**"

Except for the fact that Caryn and her boyfriend, Sal, broke down on the expressway on the way to the service causing the wedding to start 30 minutes late, there were no other hitches in our getting hitched. We couldn't start without Sal – he was taking the pictures. (He works for a photography studio and is an amateur photographer himself.) He was so rushed he didn't have time to set up his lights and tripod so the lighting in the pictures wasn't the greatest, either.

My folks were here and my brother came down from Michigan so they and my kids and their kids came back to our house that evening. Scott and I left for a four-day trip to the Smokies the next morning. We spent two nights in a chalet in the mountains outside Gatlinburg. It was a beautiful trip, especially the third day and night when we stayed at the Cataloochee Ranch in North Carolina.

If you ever get the chance, go there. You are on top of a mountain (elevation 5,000+) and can stay in one of two lodges or in individual cabins. Plus you get these family-style, made from scratch, home-cooked meals with vegetables, jams and jellies made right on the ranch. This is a working ranch, by the way. Horseback riding and buggy rides are also available and you're within 20-50 miles of all sorts of touristy things.

In early October we drove Scott's race car to Commerce, Georgia. The Atlanta GranSport Club conducted a Car Show and Drag Race on Saturday. Because his time trial was so fast – 12.88 – they made Scott race against the "trailered" cars. "Trailered" cars are those that are modified so much that they aren't allowed to run on city streets. These cars have roll bars (required) and the drivers have to wear helmets. Scott hadn't brought a helmet but was able to borrow one. Needless to say, he had a great time. And I got a kick out of him getting a kick.

We always take the back roads when we can, and did so coming back. Stopped in the beautiful little town of Dahlonega, Georgia. It claims to be the oldest mining town in the U.S. The architecture looks like you've stepped back to the 1890's.

Moving along to the present . . .

My daughter, Caryn, and Kim (John's wife) are fixing their first Christmas turkey dinner at Kim and John's – in Franklin, about 25 miles from us. We will miss Tom and Josie but the rest of my family will be together. Normally, we have holiday dinners here. But Scott and I are going on another short trip during the holidays and John, especially, wanted to have the dinner at his house. So I let them talk me into it! We may leave from Franklin in the late afternoon on Christmas Day. We're taking a scenic trip through Georgia and Alabama. When Scott was driving over the road, he marked all these places he wanted to go back and visit and this is one of them. We'll be back sometime on the 30th.

So that's it for another year. I guess one reason I continue sending these Christmas missiles is in case our travels take us through your town, I want to have a place to stay! Scott joins me in wishing you health and happiness in the year to come. A visit or a letter would be nice, of course . . . but I won't hold my breath.

Love, Sarah

8-8-92

Dear Jerry,

Thanks to you, my writing career has been launched!

The conversation we had on the phone the other day prompted me to again focus my thoughts on Rush (Limbaugh) and what he's about. The end result was the enclosed Letter to the Editor which I sent to The Tennessean.

The caption was the paper's, not mine. I would have used something like "The Archie Bunker of the '90's" or maybe, "Now THAT'S Satire".

Silly me, you can't imagine how excited I was to see my words in print. Getting calls from friends (liberal humanist quacks like me) offering congratulations and encouragement has fed my ever-expanding ego, also.

The letter got the "Three-Star" rating. I didn't know what that meant til a friend who works at the paper told me it was given to letters that were well written and timely in subject matter. Three Star winners attend a once-a-year banquet sponsored by The Tennessean. And are offered the chance to speak! Needless to say, I won't be one of them. Speaking, that is.

Of course I'm already working on my next piece – a 600 word article (paper's requirement) for the Nashville Eye column – on Pro-Choice.

And then next year, when my book is published . . .

You don't need to respond to this nonsense, Jerry. It is true, however, that you helped me write it. So I wanted to send you a copy. I thought you might be amused.

I close with loving thoughts of your family and the hope that you and they walk in health and happiness for a long, long time.

Regards, Sarah

SARAH'S STORY

Three-Star Letter to the Editor, Thursday/August 6, 1992, The Tennessean

Rush Limbaugh as a sensitive man? Hah! (Their title)

To the Editor:

An open letter of apology to Rush Limbaugh:

* * * * *

Enlightened friends and acquaintances have recently informed me that I have missed the intent of your daily program on WLAC Radio because I failed to realize you utilize satire to illustrate your points of view.

In an effort to correct my understanding of your philosophy I checked Webster's New Collegiate Dictionary, which defines "satire" as follows:

1. A poem or work of prose holding up to ridicule or scorn human vices, follies, etc.

2. Trenchant wit, irony, or sarcasm, used for the purpose of exposing and discrediting vice or folly.

Thanks goodness I checked. I now realize you are not an insensitive male chauvinist with no regard for women, other minorities, animals, or the environment.

You are not an ultra right-wing extremist, fanatic conservative after all.

You care about people, animals, and the future of this beautiful planet we call home as much as I do. And I am a senstive feminist, moderately liberal humanist. Welcome to the fold.

I apologize for misjudging you, sir.

Sarah Barnes
P.O. Box 78083 37207

December 26, 1992

T'was the day after Christmas and Sarah began preparing her cards . . .

(Just when you think you've gotten all the Christmas mail you're going to get, here comes my delightful and cheery yearly synopsis to brighten your day and shoo away those "post holiday blues". That's me, thoughtful as ever).

What was it that Queen Elizabeth recently said on nationwide TV? Something to the effect that 1992 is not a year upon which she will reflect with fondness? (Something like that, anyway.)

My sentiments exactly.

To wit, in March I lost my job. Initially, I was offered a transfer, but I declined. Next, they suggested I resign – "for your sake". Since this would have precluded unemployment compensation, again I declined. The conditions leading up to and culminating in this unhappy turn of events (beginning in November of '91) had resulted in a series of disturbing (and frightening) physical symptoms I now understand as manifestations of stress. At the time, all I knew was something was very wrong and I wasn't sure how long it would be before – or if – I would able to resume full-time employment, so I knew I needed the unemployment compensation option.

Also in November of 1991, I had begun experiencing the onset of "the silent passage" (you know, that dreaded "M" word) – mild hot flashes, nervousness, and trouble sleeping accompanied by atrocious nightmares. My gynecologist recommended ERP and I started on the smallest oral dosage (Premarin and Progestin) taken daily.

The typically menopausal systems were merely nuisances and didn't much concern me. I had never had any problems having periods and I hadn't anticipated any serious ones relative to stopping. Simultaneously, however, I had developed high blood pressure, a racing pulse, and very erratic heartbeat. My long-time steady-as-a rock blood pressure of 120/80 soared to 196/120 on one occasion

SARAH'S STORY

(that same November) and stayed at 150/160 over 85/90 for several months. To stabilize and lower my blood pressure my doctor prescribed Procardia.

In an effort to regain my health, I spent the spring and summer months walking 30 minutes every day, limiting salt intake, digging in the dirt planting flowers and shrubs, and – beginning this past October – making thrice-weekly trips to a local spa for whirlpool, steam room, and pool therapy. (My dear friend, Anne, paid for a 3-month membership in return for some typing I had done for her.)

Shortly after receiving that 196/120 b.p. reading, I began experiencing anxiety attacks (though I didn't know what they were at the time) which lasted about 45 minutes. At first they were occasional but eventually I was having several each week. For no apparent reason, I would feel a spurt of adrenalin shoot through my body, get very cold, tremble uncontrollably, and feel extremely ill. So sick you feel like you're dying and you don't much care is the only way I can explain it. Because I didn't understand what was happening or why, it was frightening and I'm sure contributed to my elevated blood pressure. The doctor prescribed a mild tranquilizer and it helped immensely. Being away from the source of stress (the job) was, of course, a major factor. As well as understanding what was happening and why.

I'm sure the blood pressure problem was a direct result of the stress I was under prior to and as a result of losing my job and merely coincidental in time with the onset of active menopause.

For the most part, the panic attacks have subsided but I still take ½ tablet almost every night because otherwise I wake up with horrible nightmares. But I hate drugs and worry about dependency.

Starting 3 medications at the same time is not too smart, either. If you develop side effects, you don't know what is causing what.

I finally stopped taking the oral hormones back in June because I constantly felt as though I had my finger stuck in an electric socket. It was as though I could feel every nerve in my body – and every one of them was "zinging". It was impossible to feel relaxed. Yet relaxing was exactly what I needed to be able to do. My body just didn't feel like my body anymore. It was as though a foreign entity had invaded it.

I didn't think I should stop taking the Procardia cold turkey (and without my doctor's direction) so I stopped the oral hormones – to see if it would make a difference. The day after I stopped, the invader left. What a relief!

From past experience with my allergies, I knew that I absorb oral medication very fast so I now think I was just getting too much too fast. Two weeks ago, I started using "the patch". I've been feeling more "electrified" again lately but hope it is just my new job plus the hectic holiday schedule. I have talked to women, however, who tried various combinations and nothing worked. They ended up feeling worse not better; I hope I'm not going to be one of them. I know I'm very susceptible to medication of any kind and need about half what someone else would take.

One other crazy thing is that, as a result of those early high blood pressure readings, I have now developed what is known as "white coat" syndrome. Which means every time I go to the doctor to have my blood pressure checked, I get very anxious – which makes the reading erroneously elevated. Round and round I go!

I know what you're thinking right about now. This is a cheery Christmas note??? You're right. On to more pleasant subjects.

In the interim of being laid off from gainful employment, I took the opportunity to pursue a subconscious life long ambition – attempting to write – for MONEY.

Last June I joined a Writers Group, and in September took a 4-week writing course. I've now finished three articles (one is about liberalism/pro-choice, one about discovering that I'm a writer[10], (not to be confused with "author" – which means published) and the third is about teenage life--fifties style[11]. The last is about

---

[10] See Prologue

[11] See Teenage Romance – Fifties Style

3000 words and I end it with a poem. I think it and the poem are excellent, naturally. It's funny and poignant and I believe it paints a typical picture of how it was "back then". I think women my age will identify with and appreciate its perspective.

I've written a couple of other poems through the years and so far I've sent the 3 articles and 3 poems to numerous publications. I've received encouragement but no acceptances yet. It's been challenging and fun, however, and I'm still hoping to make the right connection in time. I have lots more ideas and a two-foot file full of things I've written through the years which can be condensed and fine-tuned for further submissions.

Incidentally, Wayne, you're in one of them – another article about my life just prior to and including the beginning of my relationship with Jerry. (How many times did you provide me a shoulder to cry on?!). It still needs work but if I ever finish it and it gets in print, I'll be sure to send you a copy!

So far my only claim to writing fame is a Letter to the Editor which was published by The Tennessean back in August. Each day one published letter receives a "Three Star" rating for quality of content, timeliness of subject, and grammar. "Three Star" writers are invited to a once-a-year banquet held by The Tennessean and are given the option of speaking. I was the Three Star winner for August 8th. (I don't intend to speak . . . writing is hard enough.) They also sent me a check for $4.00! So, technically, I am a published writer! How about that!

After losing my job, I hoped I would be able to work part-time at home (while waiting for the royalty checks from my writing) so we traded in our Tandy Joke Of A Computer for the real thing. I now have an 80 meg hard drive computer and a color monitor with 2 meg of RAM. It's a component set so I can add and/or upgrade at any time. I still have a Tandy printer but hope to purchase a better one soon.

Two weeks ago I began working full-time once more. At Steiner-Liff, where Scott now works(*). Initially, Scott's boss, (a "computer nerd" – see below) who knew I was unemployed, asked if I would be interested in coming in part-time to help out. The second day I was there he began pressuring me to start full-time. I still don't feel completely well and would have preferred to ease back into the work force more gradually but it seemed prudent financially to take him up on his offer. Plus my unemployment compensation had run out.

So here I am. Working in Collection and Delivery at a scrap metal recycling plant. It's interesting but I have a lot to learn. I wish I could say it was not a stressful environment but I can't. Like a zoo is what it is. They operate in "crisis management" mode only. Another way of saying they have lots of problems and seem to go round and round without making headway in implementing solutions. Scott has been sharing his frustrations over their self-defeating and inept maneuvers for the past two years and now I can see for myself first-hand.

Frustrating because with his teaching and supervisory background, one of Scott's strengths is identifying problems and developing logical, efficient procedures for solving them. His responsibilities include developing and implementing maintenance and driver training procedures. Every time he approaches his immediate supervisor with his ideas, however, the man tells him, "Oh, I'm already working on that" or something similar and often takes his proposals (which we sometimes have spent several hours developing and typing here at home). Then – nothing happens. At the same time, the next level boss (the man who hired me) keeps asking Scott, "when are you going to come up with some solutions? I'm tired of hearing about the problems. I know the problems." (This is the guy I called the computer nerd – he loves them, of course. And thinks everything can be solved in a minute or two – if you just know the right buttons to push on the computer!). Not.

I've told Scott the way we get around this is to document his efforts by sending memos to his immediate supervisor listing what he's done, outlining problems he's identified, offering solutions. Then you close by saying something like, "If you wish me to assume responsibility for blah, blah, blah, please advise", or "if you wish me

SARAH'S STORY

to pursue this further, please advise". Then you copy the boss who keeps asking, "what are you doing". It's called CYA, I believe. (If this sounds like we think his immediate supervisor doesn't know what the hell he's doing, you're right).

I think I have similar abilities in understanding how to work efficiently and productively with office procedures. So who knows, maybe between the two of us, we can straighten them out!

In Utopia, that's how it would work, of course. But this company is about as far from Utopia as you can get, so we're not overly optimistic. Once I learn the ropes, if the working conditions and problems don't improve, we've agreed – I'm outta there. It's just not worth it – especially not for what they pay. The stress level is very high right now because of the problems. Yet the problems are not unsolvable. And could be solved relatively easily if the company managed from the bottom up instead of from the top down. It has too often been my experience that the people at the top don't know how to punch a staple (excuse me, Wayne, that was not directed at you!).

Here I am on page 4 and haven't mentioned my darling kids – guess I'm getting narcissistic in my old age, too.

Caryn is spending two weeks in South Carolina with a friend and using the time to "get my priorities in order". She moved back in with us a couple of months ago, though we seldom see her. She lost her office job a few months ago, too, and has been picking up shifts at TGIF's but dislikes the influence (so do I). She said she hopes to get back to an 8-5 office job after her trip.

Lisa and Steve's (**) little baby, Andrew Stephen, is 3 months and has a ton of pitch black hair! They went to Michigan for Christmas. They have opened a Kirby Dealership in Manchester, Tennessee, about 40 miles from here and have rented an office building and a 2-bedroom home located next door.

They plan to move into the house in a few more weeks. Right now they're commuting every day.

John and Kim and Jeremy are doing well and came for dinner yesterday. Caryn tells me John has a reputation for being "one of the best sound men in Nashville". Stuff like that warms a mother's heart, don't you know. He and Tom still dream of starting their own sound company one of these days.

I haven't seen Tom and Josie and their children in over a year and had planned to spend a few days between Christmas and New Year's with them. Starting the job nixed that. I'm especially anxious to see their new little baby, Thomas Henry. (Named after Grandpa Sullivan who died last November). He was born with a cleft palette but the doctors told them it was the easiest of any birth defect to correct. In fact, by the time he is school age, it should be unnoticeable. Medical technology has given society some thorny ethical issues to deal with but correcting something like this sure isn't one of them. Thank God for their expertise.

For the first time I can remember, my folks didn't drive over for Christmas. They were here at Thanksgiving and just didn't feel up to another trip again. It broke my heart. They said it was the drive but I know it's because a house full of children – big and little – no matter how well loved – is just about more than they can handle at 80 years of age. Plus, our house is quite small and there just isn't a place for them to "be"– to rest and relax. So I understand. But it's not easy to accept the realities of life sometimes.

* * * * *

Each year when I prepare to write this letter, I think – I don't know what to say. It's too much trouble. It's too late. They don't want to hear all this nonsense, anyway. Eventually, of course, I plop myself down at the computer and start.

And this is what comes out. One of these days I'll quit wearing us all out. But not today.

Even though our lives have taken divergent paths, even though we don't communicate or write as often as we should, you all are dear to me. Memories of times long past are etched inside my heart. (And etched on paper, too, because of all the crazy letters and musings I've written through the years – and saved). Eventually it will all be in my book, of course.

For now, please know I wish for you happiness and health in the coming year. I also wish for a letter. Or a visit. How about a postcard?

(We did hear from Wayne and Cora Lee, Connie and Terry, and Nan and Tom Smith. Thanks so much for not letting go.)

Love and Warm Regards,
Sarah and Scott

(*) Scott interviewed for a teaching position locally and was told he had the job so he quit his Over-The-Road truck driving job. Then the school called to say the teacher he was to replace had changed his mind and was not retiring afterall. (?!) So Scott applied and got a job in the Dispatch Office of Steiner-Liff.

(**)After being on her own again for about a year, Lisa met Steve and they set up housekeeping together in the Nashville area in early 1991; I was delighted to be present for Andrew's birth.

August 25, 1993

LIBERAL AND PROUD

In a recent Letter To The Editor in our local newspaper, (The Tennessean, Nashville, Tennessee), Gerald Hayes admonished closet liberals to stand up and be counted. Let me proudly join his ranks and proclaim myself a patriotic Liberal who espouses family values which include respect for the inherent dignity of every human being.

If you wonder why I'm proud, just check the dictionary definition of liberal/liberalism rather than listening to the sound bites of the Republican/Conservative Right.

It is the Liberals working so judiciously for the rights of all the people in our society that enable conservatives, pro-life advocates – and all others – to express their beliefs and follow their conscience in matters of ethics and morality. This seemingly self-evident concept appears to be beyond the scope of the intelligence of Right Wing Conservatives, however.

So I must pose this question to them. Do you really wish to live in a society in which the government would have the right to tell you that you MUST have an abortion? (This is a fact of life in China today – but you probably know that).

It couldn't happen here, you say. But think with me for a moment.

"Be careful what you wish for, you just might get it" may be trite, but it is also valid. Now – follow to its logical conclusion the decision to give the authority to decide the abortion issue to the government.

That logical conclusion must include the *possibility* that our future government – five, ten – twenty years from now could decide not only is abortion going to be legal, it is going to be mandatory.

To pose a hypothetical possibility, mandatory abortion could be required for women with more than two children, or even with one child if overpopulation and food shortages continue. In an effort to control population and food supply, the government could conceivably expand mandatory abortion for all single women and/or all women under twenty, for example. Or even issue a complete moratorium on all births for a specified period of time.

To carry the logical conclusion further, once the government is given the authority to dictate our morality over one issue – in this case, abortion – we embark upon a slippery slope that could easily end in theocratic fascism. Surely we'll never stop recoiling in horror from Nazi Germany – a right-wing, anti-abortion, God-Fearing, Christian nation – run amuck!

It seems self-evident to me that Pro-Life advocates and religious conservatives would support and defend the so-called "liberal position" with all their might. It is the existence of this very concept that ensures they have the right to choose to give life if they become pregnant, to practice their religion as their conscience dictates, and to express their views accordingly.

These choices have been ensured – thus far in our society – because of the diligence of the liberal thinkers who are the guardians and protectors of these precious freedoms. Thus, it is **because** I am a liberal that I respect and defend the rights of pro-life advocates and conservatives to make their moral and ethical choices. I just wish they could understand the need to respect and defend mine.

In conclusion, I postulate the following: It is entirely possible to be conservative in our personal choices – with regard to issues such as abortion, morality, religion, ethics, etc. and yet embrace the "liberal" philosophy which recognizes that the ethics and morality of *each* citizen is a precious yet precarious commodity which must be vigilantly defended and protected. I know it's possible . . . it's what I do.

So come on, closet liberals, join ranks with Gerald Hayes and me. Speak up. (That makes two – and counting).

December 23, 1993

Merry Christmas!

Hope you all are well and enjoying the holiday activities with family and friends.

Until yesterday, I was expecting all my kids – and their kids – plus my mom and dad to be here Christmas Eve and Day. But then Lisa and my folks called to say they couldn't make it. (Lisa doesn't think her car is safe to drive on a 7-hour trip plus now she says Mo and Steve are coming for turkey dinner. That should be fun! My folks "just don't feel up to it".). It would have been the first Christmas since 1981 that we were all together.

Tom, Josie, and children arrived at 3 a.m. this morning. They "arrived" at Kim and John's. John and Kim will be going to Kim's relatives for Christmas Eve. Everyone else will come here. Caryn is cooking spaghetti. Then everyone will be back here for dinner Christmas Day. Our little house will be pretty full but we're all looking forward to sharing this time together. I just wish my folks, Lisa, Leila, and Andrew could make it fuller.

Sunday morning, Scott and I and Randy and Caryn are driving to Gatlinburg for three days. In late November Caryn still managed to find accommodations and reserved a two-bedroom suite at The Summit which is located on a mountain overlooking the city. Plus it has a sofa bed in the living room so Kim and John and Jeremy are coming up Monday. Plus it has an indoor pool, whirlpool and sauna (so everyone knows where to go looking for mom when she disappears). Originally, Caryn and Randy planned to ski but I think they've nixed that idea now. We'll leave for home on Wednesday.

Tom and Josie are still living in Royal Oak, Michigan with their three children – Sammy Jo (7), Carrie Michelle (5+), and little Thomas Henry (1 year plus). Tom began working for Roush Industries as a prototype mechanic a few months ago. They produce prototypes for the automotive industry. They still have hopes of moving down here within a year or two so that John and Tom can start up their own sound company here in Nashville.

John, Kim, and Jeremy still roam the country on the Jessie bus. This is their slow period. John also drives for Louise Mandrell from time to time and does sound work locally with other musicians during slack periods. Caryn recently told me he has a reputation for being "one of the best sound men" in the business. (Did I say that last year? Oh, well, proud moms are allowed.) That surprised me (shame on me!) but also made me very proud, of course. Kim was signed to a recording contract this past year and has completed the studio work. It is not a major label – but it is a start – so we're thrilled and excited for her. She had to have some publicity photos made and after much thoughtful consideration came up with the stage name of Riley Sullivan. For many reasons, we all agreed it was the perfect choice.

Lisa, Leila (4), and Andrew (2) moved from Chattanooga and Steve to Richmond, Kentucky, several months ago. She is working in the office of a Kirby Distributorship there in Richmond and recently found an apartment in Berea, Kentucky.

She is struggling but determined as always. There is a song, "Wildflower", by a group called Skylark. Some of the words are:

"She's faced the hardest times you could imagine
And many times her eyes fought back the tears
And when her youthful world was about to fall in
Each time her slender shoulder
Bore the weight of all her fear
And sorrow no one hears
Still rings in midnight silence in her ears...
The way she's always paying
For a debt she doesn't owe . . .

Let her cry for she's a lady
Let her dream for she's a child . . .

I gave her a copy for her birthday. It's how I think of her. I love her very much.

Caryn became Mrs. Randall Johnson last September. Mothers are allowed to say – "she was a beautiful bride" and they don't have to apologize – so I do and don't. They went to Florida for a 3-day honeymoon. She has been working as an Administrative Assistant at Liberty Records for the past couple of months. Initially, it was a temporary job but she is expecting it to become permanent after the first of the year. Randy was recently promoted to Steward at Fridays and spends his spare time writing and studying music. They both believe he has a special calling for contemporary Christian music. He's been writing and playing music since his teens and is optimistic about publishing.

I've been working at Steiner-Liff Iron & Metal Co. just over a year now but switched to their night shift – and 30 hours – about three months ago. I go in at 4 p.m. and stay till I finish – sometimes 10 p.m., sometimes 11:30 p.m. I like it much better especially since they allowed me to keep full-time benefits. The day shift is chaotic, frustrating, and stressful. In the evening I work pretty much undisturbed. I keep my radio tuned to WPLN (the local public radio station which plays some really neat stuff at night) or Easy Listening.

Scott left S/L two months ago. He took another over-the-road driving job with a company that runs teams. It lasted two days. On his last day of work at Steiner-Liff he injured his back (again). Hoping it would go away, he and his new team driver left from their new terminal the following Sunday evening. By Tuesday he could barely walk and had to leave the company truck in Ohio.

He took a commercial bus back to Nashville. His leg and toes were numb and he had shooting pains up and down his leg. The doctor said he had a pinched nerve.

Because it happened the last day he worked at S/L he was able to collect Workman's Comp and spent the next six weeks under that coverage – thank goodness. He's pretty well recovered and is trying to decide what to do. He's still thinking of over-the-road but also looking into other possibilities, one of which is buying a van and getting into the Courier business.

He's written several articles for a friend who has a Buick parts business and sends a monthly newsletter to 5500 subscribers. Scott gets 3-4 calls a month from men from all over the country who read his articles and want more information or advice. So he's toying with the idea of starting a mail order catalogue business.

He would write articles (some of which are already written) that identify problems/solutions for Buick car owners (especially geared to antique car owners). Each article would offer car part kits for fixing the problems. He would contract with a local supplier to provide the parts to him wholesale.

He would then advertize in various mail order catalogues, especially those directed to Buick owners. The Buick Club of America and the Antique Car Club of America have thousands of members so I think there is a viable market. It's a business that wouldn't require much investment and that's an important consideration.

One of the reasons I like the mail order business idea so much is that it would tie in with my desire to run a home-based typing service. If he was to produce these articles I would have to type and print them. We would need to buy a good printer and I would probably also buy a DeskTop Publishing software package for the computer. This would enable me to offer typing services, particularly Newsletter typing services.

Plus I haven't given up my writing ambitions either. Last year I think I mentioned I'd written three articles – Liberal and Proud, Teenage Romance – Fifties Style, and So That's It (an article I wrote about discovering I was a writer). Except for a Letter to the Editor I wrote about Rush Limbaugh, no one is beating down my door with offers – yet. I've drafted another article, "A Child of the Forties" which it isn't complete. And still have tons of notes, ideas, etc. to get to "someday".

All my writing fits the genre of "articles from the heart", which means it's based on personal experiences, hopefully with a touch of humor and/or pathos. Either I haven't found the right market or I'm not very good. I prefer to think it's the former. So I'm not discouraged – yet.

Anyway, if what I read and see on TV is accurate (and who knows), home-based businesses are the wave of the '90's. Mr./Mrs. Average America has learned the hard way that loyalty to the company isn't reciprocated so it seems a logical/protective alternative.

Well, as usual, I sat down without knowing what to say and then said it and said it and said it. Which is what makes me a writer. Which is not the same as author, of course.

One of these days when our ship comes in, we'll be rich and famous and living in our dream log house on five acres in the country and we'll have lots of room for kids and grandkids and friends. And you'll all come and visit.

One of these days.

In the meantime, in the real world, we still think of you, treasure our memories of days and times past, and hope that opportunities to meet again are just over the horizon. And that each day of the coming year will at the least contain acceptance and peace and at the best joy and happiness.

Love, Sarah

SARAH'S STORY

Sarah Jensen
XXX Xxxxxx Xxxxxxx, Nashville, TN XXXXX
(615) XXX-XXXX, (615) 228-3714 (fax)

Professional Typing Service
Reasonable Rates

November 4, 1994

PAWS
P.O. Box 849
Galt, CA 95632

Dear PAWS:

Enclosed is the letter and the list of veterinarians to whom I sent it with regard to the chaining and abuse of elephants in circuses and zoos.

I'm so happy to be in a position to devote a little of my time and energy to such a worthy cause. Even though I'm in my first year of self-employment and money and lack of benefits is a concern right now as a result, the fact that I am working at home has allowed me to pursue this endeavor. If I were working full-time in an office, it would be more difficult to find the time and energy. I've always been an advocate of animal rights and it's great to have a chance to "put my money where my mouth is," so to speak.

I hope the efforts of us all will have some positive results in achieving freedom and humane treatment for the animals of this world who cannot speak for themselves.

You may recall a series of televised interviews Bill Moyers conducted with Joseph Campbell a few years ago. In one of them Joseph Campbell suggested we use our wisdom and energy to promote a world in which everything in it – people, plants, and animals – is valued as a "thou" rather than an "it". Let's hope our efforts result in raising the consciousness of large numbers of people to this end.

Sincerely,
Sarah Jensen, (encls)

Sarah Jensen
XXX Xxxxxx Xxxxxxx, Nashville, TN XXXXX
(615) XXX-XXXX, (615) 228-3714 (fax)

Professional Typing Service
Reasonable Rates

November 4, 1994

Dear Animal Lover:

Two weeks ago "The Crusaders" (Channel 2, Sunday evenings) aired an investigative report showing elephants and a whale going "berserk", killing and/or injuring their trainers. The piece went on to describe the physical abuse these animals have been subjected to which resulted in their aggressive and destructive behavior. They had an edited film clip (edited because the extent of the abuse they had filmed was deemed too graphic to show on TV) showing two elephant trainers hitting an elephant repeatedly with a baseball bat on his head and feet and whacking him again and again with a long prod that looked like the hook worn by Captain Hook in the fabled Peter Pan children's classic. It was sickening and obscene.

You and/or your clients may not be as ignorant of this abuse as I was. I naively assumed that the men and women who worked with circus animals loved them and taught them to perform in the same way I have trained my dogs, by repeating simple instructions over and over and rewarding their animals with food and affection. What a shock to learn how mistaken I was.

I am writing you at this time to solicit your assistance in helping to stop this abuse. I have enclosed several petitions and ask that you encourage your patrons to sign them. Please return the petitions to me when you get as many signatures as possible. I realize this will take several weeks. I am writing all veterinarians in the Nashville area with this request. In addition, I plan to contact other organizations and groups in an effort to obtain as much support as possible.

If any of your patients' owners are interested in getting more information, they can call (916) 393-PAWS. If you need more copies of the petition, and can run them on your copier that would be wonderful; however, I would be happy to send additional copies if you need them.

I appreciate your assistance in this manner.

Sincerely,

Sarah Jensen
encls

This letter sent to 100 veterinarians in Metropolitan Nashville area

Post Script to PAWS Letter and Petition –
Shortly after airing this segment, The Crusaders just "disappeared" from the TV programming. One week it was on, the next it was gone.

A few weeks later I called PAWS to see if they knew anything about the cancellation and their representative told me that Disney Studios had the program canceled. At that time, Disney owned Ringling Bros circuses.

Interesting.

December 1994 Update:
One local area veterinary clinic returned one petition with about 15 names. I forwarded to PAWS.

December 15, 1994

Happy Christmas and Merry New Year Greetings from Nashville!

It's that time again each year when I set with computer in hand (that's pen, circa 1955) pondering over the events of the past year trying to think of a way to make them sound interesting. Somehow the words always come, though whether or not they're interesting may be debatable. Anyway, I try.

So. We're looking forward to Christmas dinner at Kim and John's (Caryn and John are cooking, although I graciously offered to make the dressing) on Christmas Day. My folks declined to drive here for Thanksgiving (I cooked – ?) and say they don't feel able to come for Christmas either. In speaking to them recently on the phone, Daddy kept saying it was too cold. I finally figured out he wasn't talking about the weather – he was talking about the temperature in my house!

Kim is working full-time at Home Depot and giving radio interviews in connection with her album, <u>Country in my Jeans</u>, (on the Playback Label under the name "Riley Sullivan"). It's not a major label, but most music outlets carry it. She tells us it's getting a lot of air play overseas.

John has been with Gopher-It Sound Company for the past five months or so. He's thrilled because his only responsibility is running sound, which he loves. The job came about as a result of a friend recommending him to the owner of the company. (The owner later told John's friend, "George, you deserve a medal for putting me in touch with John."). Still on the road, of course, but instead of Jessie, he's working with groups like The Kentucky Headhunters, Lee Greenwood, Sha-Na-Na, Patti Loveless, etc. In between gigs, he continues to drive for Louise Mandrell.

Caryn and Randy are happy and busy. Caryn has been with the Securities Division of First American for about three months now (she went there as a "Temp" with Jane Jones and of course they recognized her talent and intelligence immediately). Randy works for Air Express International, a commercial shipping and receiving company.

With regard to his music, he's nearly completed his first demo (record) and hopes that a Christian recording company will soon recognize his talent, too. They live about five miles away so we see them often and Caryn and I toddle off to the spa two or three times a week.

Tom and Josie and their children are still in Michigan. Little Tommy recently had more surgery on his face. By school-age, they expect the surgeries to be successfully completed. Tom left his job with Rosh Industries several months ago (the work was bor--ing) and went back to Shear's Gas Station but they are closing this location in March.

He called last week to tell us he has the chance to go into business with a man who has had a radiator shop for the past fourteen years, wants to expand his base of operation, and has asked Tom to come in with him. Tom has had business dealings with the man for several years and believes he is an honest, up-front guy so he's pretty excited about the opportunity. We are all happy for him, of course, even though this makes the possibility of their eventually moving to Tennessee less likely.

Lisa, Leila, and Andrew are back in Michigan with Mo; he drove down in the spring to get them. He leased a tri-level house in Warren. Steve eventually followed her up there and continues to harass her one way or another but I'm hoping she can hang in there with Mo and keep some semblance of stability for herself and her precious little children.

The lower level of the house has a family room, kitchen, and bath which is ideal for a day care facility, so she got one started about a month ago. She has three children part of every day plus one baby all day. Needless to say, it keeps her hopping. Leila is in kindergarten now and was talking to Caryn on the phone recently, telling her about school and how early she has to get up. Caryn asked her, "well, honey, how early is that?" "Oh, real early. One o'clock in the morning," she said.

Scott has been driving locally for DOT Leasing since last December. Two months ago he got a call from the superintendent of Metro schools asking him to interview for a teaching position. At the last minute, the teacher changed his mind about leaving (this same thing happened in 1992!).

Of course, we were really excited – the superintendent had told Scott he was their top candidate – and very disappointed when it fell through. The only hopeful thing about the whole situation is that the superintendent was really impressed with Scott and told him he was anxious to add him to his teaching staff one way or another. He did say two vocational teachers will be retiring at the end of this school year – but, who knows. The recent election outcome could very easily have a negative effect on the public school system and if money gets tight, one of the first places to feel the squeeze is the Vocational Ed department. So for now, he's hanging in with DOT and we're hoping for the best.

I mentioned in last year's letter that he's written a series of articles for a Buick performance newsletter that a friend of his publishes in connection with his Buick parts business. The response has been really good. As a result, two people have contacted Scott with the idea of writing a book. Each is kind of an expert in two or three areas so the idea is that each one will write what he knows and they will combine it in a technical, 'how-to' book for people interested in racing and performance. So he's excited about this possibility even though the market is, understandably, limited.

We took our first big-time, go-for-broke vacation last July – to Florida. (We didn't really plan it that way, but when we added up the cost later, we agreed that definitely is the category it would fall in). We stopped the first night in Gainesville. When I turned on the television, I learned that Florida was in the midst of Hurricane

Alberto. I could not believe that here I was on my first – and probably only – trip to Florida and I was about to be swept away in a hurricane! I finally calmed down when Scott explained the storm was on the opposite side of the state.

Scott's half-sister lives in Tequesta. We spent a couple of days with her and her husband and then had a delightful 4th of July cookout with Connie and Terry West, who just happened to be spending the week at a condo on the ocean about five miles from his sister's. Then we headed up to St. Augustine where we did the regular tourist thing, cramming as much as possible into a three-day stay there before heading back home. What a beautiful and historically exciting city.

I loved the ocean and during the trip and for about two weeks after, every time I lay down to sleep, I saw, felt, and heard the ocean – it was wonderful. But not unique, I guess; others have since told me they reacted similarly after being exposed to the ocean for a few days' time.

My one disappointment was that everywhere we went to eat I asked for "ocean perch" – I mean, what more likely place for ocean perch than at the ocean, right? Wrong. Not one restaurant had it. Some servers even gave me quizzical looks when I asked for it. I did finally get my perch, though – at Kroger's in Nashville – on the Saturday we returned home!

Upon returning to my part-time job at Steiner-Liff, I was confronted with a situation I deemed untenable – so I quit. My first day back (evening shift) on Friday was also my last. Liberation, how sweet it is.

So I started my home-based typing service. I had purchased WP60 for DOS and a laser printer in the Spring so all I needed were some clients.

A good friend of mine is a court reporter and she had been typing for a photo journalist. She was having to pass up more lucrative work in order to accommodate this individual so she asked if I would like to take over. I jumped at the chance, of course, even though the pay is atrocious.

The woman is an extremely imaginative and talented photographer, Maria von Matthiessen by name, and her first book, "Songs From The Hills," is a beautiful book of photographs of country music characters (one of which is Jessie, by the way). She travels all over the country interviewing wonderful characters that live 'off the beaten path' but still are famous for their lifestyles, crafts, etc. From the interviews that I transcribe for her, she writes stories to accompany the photographs. Then I type up the stories, plus letters, proposals, etc., whatever she needs.

Her priority project right now is called, "A Year of Seeing Country in the South," and will include stories and photos of people like song writer John Laudermilk (you may remember one of his hits from the Fifties – "A Rose and a Baby Ruth"), now semi-retired on his farm in Christiana, Tennessee. He takes all visitors out to see his Chinkipin Oak (the largest in Tennessee) which is eighteen feet around and 70 feet high. How you relate to his tree determines whether your visit is a short or long one (I love it!).

Then there's the southern writer, Eudora Welty; Maria has written a story about her and her home from a cricket's point of view. And Jamie Wilson, part Ojibwa Indian, a retired rodeo clown (at 33), who sculpts animals from old bone and stone that is sent to him from people around the world. He lives in the country near Lebanon, Tennessee, and works from a trailer filled with stone and wood. A successful friend of his offered to set him up in a studio on Second Avenue; he declined, saying the confines of such a studio would stifle his creativity. And Mary Simms, an eccentric painter in Eureka Springs, Arkansas; and 88-year-old Mildred Huie, St. Simons Island, Georgia, an historical writer who also makes life-size dolls (has been interviewed by Dan Rather) to travel with people who are traveling alone. So you can see why I am fascinated with this on-going project.

SARAH'S STORY

Maria herself is quite a character. According to what she's told me, her father was a German count and she roamed the rooms of European castles in her early childhood, although her family migrated to New York City at some point in her childhood. As she tells it, a few years ago she was overseas and drank some orange juice into which a youngster had poured some kind of cleaning solvent.

As a result, she says her 'intestines leak' (?), and she is fighting to regain her health. She needs constant assistance in order to perform her work and has two assistants who travel with her plus work with her when she's here in Nashville. It's almost a 24-hour-a-day job. Initially, she asked Scott and me to fill this spot. Even though it would be exciting and interesting, it would also be extremely demanding and she can't afford (she says) to pay enough to make it worth our while. So, instead, I stay here and type for her. When not taking photographs, she spends much of her time in a wheelchair.

Like all creative people, I guess, her imagination gets the best of her and with regard to her health she is absolutely paranoid. Scott spent one day with her here in Nashville when she had a photo session down on Riverfront Park. One of his assignments that day was to go to Wal-Mart and buy 30 shower heads. Her fear of germs requires her to shower twice a day – each time with a new shower head!

But her work is wonderful. Spiritually and otherwise I am very much drawn to what she is attempting to say with her photographs and stories.

In addition to Maria, I transcribe tapes for my court reporter friend, mostly depositions. She also works for <u>The Tennessean</u> (one of Nashville's major papers) and has asked me to fill in for her on occasion. I was at the paper two Friday nights in a row just before the elections, when Channel 2 carried two "Meet The Candidates" town meetings. I transcribed tapes verbatim, which were really 'back-up' for the reporters who were covering the program. It was interesting but I wouldn't want to work that way all the time. Deadlines are constant and I was typing as fast and furiously as I could for four plus hours each night. (Carpel tunnel – virtual reality).

I have another client who is a court reporter and she recently called and told me Liberty Records (who represent Garth Brooks) called and asked her to recommend a typist for a rush job they had. Guess who she suggested? When she told me what they paid, I jumped at the chance, of course. So, little by little, I'm expanding my network and base of operations.

I still try to write but haven't had much time to pursue it seriously. I have written several poems in the past few months, however, and discovered that, in some ways, it's easier than writing prose. You don't have to worry about grammar, or the 'beginning, middle, and end', and you don't have to compose consistent, logical sentences and paragraphs. You just write what you feel. 'Explaining' is actually counter-productive. If the words are right, they explain themselves.

A song I heard on the radio a few months ago as I was typing for Maria inspired a poem about my parents. Shortly after that I took the time to pull out my thoughts about Lisa that had been rumbling around in my head ever since Caryn's wedding. As Lisa stood there in front of me that day, I looked at her shoulders revealed in the cranberry, off-the-shoulder dress she was wearing and my heart wrenched inside me. Those tender shoulders looked so vulnerable; not nearly strong enough to bear the weight of responsibility they carried. So, a poem was born. And that led to three more, of course; one for each of my other precious progeny.

So, one thing leads to another and I manage to keep busy. In fact, I have to force myself to take breaks from time to time – to walk, use my stair-stepper, or go to the spa for 'rejuvenation therapy'. All things considered, I love it. Of course, neither Scott nor I presently have any medical insurance or other benefits, and that is not a happy thought. If he gets a teaching position next year, we'll be able to breathe a little easier. In the meantime, we take our vitamins, try to exercise, and think positive.

Speaking of thinking positive, I'm going to do so by thinking that all of you will write me back and fill me in on what's going on in your lives – and I'm going to project that positive thinking even further to include our hope that you put Nashville on your trip list this next year.

In the interim, each of you has a special place in my heart that neither time nor distance can erode and Scott and I send loving thoughts for your happiness and health in the coming year.

Love, Sarah

December 1995

Merry Christmas and Happy New Year
To Dear Old Friends and Family
from Scott and Sarah Jensen

I'm turning over a new leaf this year. So this will be short and sweet. That's because I spent the time I should have been using writing this letter writing something else. I'm not sure what it is, an essay, I guess, and I've enclosed a copy. I thought you might enjoy it. It's something I do from time to time when the spirit moves me. Last year I wrote a poem for each of my children and one for my parents.

Most of my time is spent typing depositions for court reporters. Plus I've been working with two "writers" on their manuscripts, typing and editing for them. I say writers, not authors. Neither has yet been published. (One never will.) I'm hoping to start tutoring children on the computer after the first of the year. There are several good computer programs available which teach computer skills while also teaching math, science, etc. I just bought a program that teaches typing and plan to start with that as a pilot program. We have several families with children right here on our street and I'm going to test the waters by putting flyers in their mailboxes offering my services. There are two schools within walking distance and I may contact them as well.

Scott is back over-the-road with PTL (Paschal Truck Lines). He hired on in August and after three months we once again got medical insurance (having been without for two years). But the lifestyle is a killer. He's having too many health problems so he's going to look for something else after the first of the year. A couple of months ago, he got sick while on the road and ended up in the hospital overnight. Before the insurance kicked in. Of course.

Caryn and Randy are going to North Carolina for Christmas with his dad. John, Kim, and Jeremy are making a mad dash for their Michigan Christmas by leaving here Christmas Eve as soon as Kim gets off work (Home Depot) and will be back on the 28th. Lisa, Leila, and Andrew are doing the best they can. She works part-time at a restaurant in a mall near her home. I think Mo helps from time to time. Steve moved to Kentucky. For now. Tom started his own mechanic shop this last year. I think he's doing okay with it. I know they are all looking forward to their usual big Sullivan family Christmas at Jerry and Nancy's.

So I decided we'd have Christmas on New Years. That way, two sets of kids can be here anyway. My folks really aren't able to make the drive themselves so if they'll let me, I'll drive down and bring them over for a few days. My dad bought a studio program for his computer which allows him to take old 8mm movie film and convert it to video. It allows you to make titles and graphics and add music in the background. It's amazing. Needless to say, this keeps him off the streets and out of trouble. Mom, bless her sweet, gentle soul, continues along the path of forgetfulness that is inevitable with her disease.

Well, I said this would be short, so I'll close by wishing you all the very best of health and happiness in the coming year. And, as always, extend our offer to show you around our booming, up-and-coming city if ever you decide to head this way.

Love, Sarah

Enclosed Essay -- "A House Full of Kids"

A House Full of Kids

As I sat signing my Christmas cards this evening, I came across a card I'd received from Joyce McGowan, a dear neighbor from another time, another place. Another me.

I noted she had moved from Vernon Avenue in Huntington Woods, Michigan, where we had lived as neighbors for so many years. Her husband, Mickey, died a few years ago but I never imagined she would move, and I wrote a note to say, "Take care, dear old friend". Unexpectedly, my eyes filled with tears. They splattered on the words that I had written as images of her house, that beautiful old house across the street from ours, blocked out the present.

The images continued, the years fell away, and I was back there once again.

It seemed to be summer and the sun was shining. Everything looked so bright. The huge old trees that lined the street were laden with foliage, the well-cared-for lawns were lush with deep green grass, and the sky was startlingly blue. The picture in my mind was of our street as though I was looking out from my house to hers.

I didn't actually see her but she was there. In her house full of kids. And I was there. In my house full of kids. We were friendly, borrowing neighbors and our kids played together and got into trouble together.

And I wondered why it had so often seemed so hard at the time to be there in that house full of kids. Then it seemed that the cares of the day often overwhelmed me. So many little hands and feet and mouths to wash, to dress, to feed. Too many dishes and clothes to wash, too many dinners to cook, too much dust to sweep, too many trips to Krogers, to the doctors, to the school, too many . . . not enough me.

Funny how time puts a different perspective on things. If I could be there right now, today, somehow I would find the patience to do it better this time. This time I would know to just hold those little kids and hug them tight and tell them how precious they were to me. Every day. Several times a day.

Today it would be such fun to gather them in the tub and wash their sturdy little bodies. I would relish the feel of their wonderfully tender skin as I rinsed and dried them with a big fluffy towel. And once again I would kiss them in that delightful, most vulnerable spot right where their neck and shoulders meet.

Today it would be such a joy to help them get ready for bed. Each one a different age, a different size. Each one needing a little more or less of mommy's helping hand. And then I would set them on the couch, my four little stair-step cherubs. And we would read some bedtime stories. Then, as I tucked each one into bed with one special song, I would give them one last kiss and hug as I listened to them say their prayers.

I did those things back then, of course. But not always so joyfully.

*****

As I sit here at my dining room table signing Christmas cards in 1995 remembering my dear old friend and the lives we lived back then, it seems like it must have been the loveliest, most wonderful thing I can think of . . .

To have lived in Huntington Woods . . .

in Michigan, . . .

in a house full of kids.

Summer 1996

– THE REUNION (*) –

As she said her goodbyes, hugging her high school chums and exchanging e-mail addresses, she thought back to the events of the day and how she had almost missed this wonderful party.

* * * * *

They had raced down Woodward Avenue, her husband visibly agitated remembering his own disappointment when job commitments prevented him from attending his 35th high school reunion a few years ago. After coming all this way, he sure didn't want his wife to miss her 40th.

A luncheon with her high school sweetheart had run longer than planned and they returned to her son's home 45 minutes before the party was to begin. The woman rushed to change clothes while her husband and her son's wife attempted to contact someone who could give them directions to the party which was being held on a river boat on the Detroit River.

What a frustrating experience *that* had been. The daughter-in-law called Information and promptly spent the next 15 minutes on hold while her husband flipped through the yellow pages, looking up "boats," "restaurants," "cruises." What kind of city doesn't have a white pages listing for their metropolitan area, he thought. Luckily, they had a second phone and he finally made connections with Stroh's River Place and hurriedly wrote down the instructions he was given.

"We could just take Woodward Avenue all the way down to the river," the woman said. "No, no; you can't do that," replied her daughter-in-law. "You can't drive through Detroit that way any more. The only way to go from the suburbs to the river is to take the expressway. In-between is a War Zone."

"I find that hard to believe," thought the woman as they hurried out the door, but she wasn't in a position to argue at this point and her husband's instructions did take them down the freeway.

It was well past six when they reached the Lodge Freeway. It was closed. Her husband's anxious tone revealed his growing concern. "Oh, my god, we'll never make it. I have no idea where to go from here," he said.

"Not to worry," said his wife. If you can get us back to Woodward from here, it's a straight shot to the river. Then we'll just turn, which way I'm not sure, and ask someone where Joseph Campau is."

They reached the river without incident although each time they stopped at a red light, the two occupants glanced uneasily at the cars around them. "It makes me mad to give in to this paranoia," she told her husband, "but when you've been away from a place this long, you buy into the rumors."

It made her even madder to think she was afraid to go and visit her old neighborhood and grade school over by State Fair and Woodward. This would be the first time since she'd moved to Tennessee that she'd come back for a visit and not gone there. It had always been something she needed to do.

That beautiful old school was still in use the last time she was here but she knew one of these days it would be gone. She loved it because of her own good memories but it had taken on an added importance when she learned her dad had gone there too back in 1919 when he lived just four houses down from her own childhood home.

Shabby though they may be, she wanted to get pictures of her old house, her street, the school. Dull and grey and gloomy, she would get an artist to render them in the vibrant colors of her child's eye.

Her husband's voice brought her attention back to the present. "Okay, here's the river. Now which way?" "Let's try left," she replied. She remembered the name Joseph Campau but really had no idea where in the city it might be. After driving a few blocks, they pulled into a convenience/gas station and she got additional directions. "We did good," she said. "Joseph Campau is just a few blocks further."

Minutes later they found the street and turned towards the river. They could see two boats at the dock and cars were inching their way forward towards a gate keeper who seemed to be taking tickets and/or money. They pulled into the parking lot to the right of the gate. There it was. The Diamond Belle. "I can't believe we made it," said her husband. "You got us here, honey, after all," she replied as she grabbed the duffle bag containing her camera, tape recorder, and about 20 other "necessary" items.

Kissing him on the cheek, she hurriedly rushed from the car towards the boat visibly listing to the left as she walked by the weight of the bulky bag.

The rear of the boat pulled away from the dock the instant her foot stepped onto the boat. Two sets of arms reached out to steady her as she crossed the gangplank. Looking up, she recognized the smiling face of Jim Hoppin who said, "Welcome aboard." Hearing other voices, she looked beyond him to the sounds of cheers and clapping from her classmates as one of her best friends from high school approached and gave her a welcoming hug.

The party had begun.

* * * * *

The story *would* have had a more dramatic ending if I'd been five minutes later. Jim told me they had given instructions to Bill's second boat to continue to wait for me. When I arrived they were to radio the Diamond Belle and arrange a ron-de-vouz somewhere in the middle of the Detroit River as they transferred their cargo, me, to the party boat.

Uh-huh!

(*) This delightful party took place ON the Detroit River, on a tour boat, The Diamond Belle, owned and operated by a classmate, Bill Hoey.

Well, not Exactly . . .

JOURNAL ENTRY 9/24/96
(After returning from 40th high school reunion)

Just got back from our Michigan trip last night. A lot of things and feelings are rumbling around in my head. So I have to write them down.

One of the things I was thinking about today was seeing all these people and enjoying it so much and thinking about the lives we've lived and the fact that we've all had our share of good times and bad and some of us, I guess, have had more bad times than good, and that may be why some of those people didn't show up, and I was especially thinking about them.

So I just started praying, "Lord, I hope you watch over them and take care of them and if they're having a really hard time in their lives, please help them get through it."

Of course, then I got to thinking about the fact that just because they didn't show up at our reunion doesn't necessarily mean they're having a hard time now. And I was reminded of what Jim Hoppin told me one day last week on the phone. He said some people probably didn't show up just because they did not **want** to show up; because maybe, unlike him and me, they don't have fond memories of dear old Lincoln High School. So that makes me feel sad too. Even though I know that's just the way kids are; they do mean things sometimes.

(After our reunion dinner, we had asked each person present to get up and tell us what he/she had been doing since graduating from dear old LHS. Several of us took pictures and I had my tape recorder set up near the mike to record their comments. I typed it all up later and sent to Jim to compile in a reunion booklet.)

I missed getting to talk to Judy and Julie as much as I would have liked. This whole reunion thing has done something weird to me. For some reason it seems like every time I think about anything, I start to cry. But the thing is I really would have liked to have spent more time with them and talked with them more about what's been going on in their lives. Judy drove Julie and me back home after the party. And I'm embarrassed to say I talked the whole time; they hardly said anything. In my defense, they kept asking me question after question. The trouble is, writers talk almost as much as they write. So I seldom give a yes/no answer to a question. I have to explain my whole life in that answer. I think that's what I did and why there wasn't much time for them to say anything. But. . .

I look at their pictures (from the reunion) and think it looks like they have had good lives.

I've always admired Julie and Jim and the way it seems they've managed their affairs. It seems to me they have been successful living their lives and raising their family. Maybe they are financially successful, too, but I'm not talking about that, I'm talking about the way they have always seemed to have their lives in order. (Which I surmise from the Christmas letters we have frequently exchanged through the years.)

And I think probably Judy and Hugh did the same. Of course, when Judy got up to talk that night I started to cry when she said Hugh passed away a few years ago, from cancer.

The big thing that made me sad about being with Julie and Judy – other than the fact that I didn't get to spend as much time with them as I would have liked – is I realized that the same kind of concern over being with them is the same kind of concern I sometimes have with my daughter, Caryn.

And it is this: with people I care about – and in this case people I used to be close friends with so I still care about them but I really don't know them anymore – these folks – and me – we've all become the people that we are going to be, you know?

Well, maybe we'll change a little more as we get even older but, basically, we already are who it is we are going to become. At this age, mostly we've reached our potential, whatever it was, and now, hopefully, we're just going to relax a little and go with the flow. Whatever mountains we had to climb, mostly I think we've climbed them.

Basically, we have become whoever it is that we're going to be. I have gone in a certain direction; other's have gone in other directions. Greatly influenced by the experiences/events we have encountered along our life path. When Scott and I were driving home I tried to explain this to him; I think he understood, and I think I'm saying something worth saying. Maybe not.

But I'm writing it down anyway.

Something that distresses me, with my children, for instance, or with someone I care about, when we get to talking about something other than the weather and how was your day; when we get to talking about the things that mean so much to each of us, maybe the things that make us who we are, our belief system, or whatever – I have this difficulty with my daughter and I sense that I would have had it with Julie and Judy if I had spent more time with them.

When I talk about who I am and what I believe with people I care about the most, it frequently seems as though a tension fills the air. An uncomfortableness settles in. I sense that they do not agree – which I have no problem with – but I get the impression they feel threatened or uncomfortable by what I am saying. I was afraid that would happen if I spent more time with Julie and Judy. I was concerned there were subjects that, if I expressed my opinion, somehow it would either offend them or make them uncomfortable. Or make me uncomfortable. As if my choice somehow negated their choice.

Certain people make me feel that if I have a point of view that's different from theirs that somehow by stating my opinion, I'm finding fault with theirs. Which is not the case. The world I live in is not necessarily one of "if I'm right, you're wrong", or vice-versa.

I have this problem sometimes with my daughter, Caryn. We often talk about spiritual things. Sometimes I am trying to explain to her how I got to be where I am spiritually or I sometimes try to share

SARAH'S STORY

something I've seen on TV, maybe a public television program, or Discovery, that I found spiritually uplifting.

For instance, Bill Moyers recently interviewed Huston Smith in a 5-part Special entitled, "The Wisdom of Faith". This man has been a religious spokesperson in our society for all of his life now.

His parents were missionaries to China when he was a little boy and I think they lived there most of his growing up years. It's only been since he's been an adult that he's come back to this country. He is a Professor of Religion at Syracuse University in New York.

He himself is a Methodist. So he personally embraces the Christian faith. But growing up in China like he did, he learned so much about that culture and that belief system, it triggered him to learn about other cultures and other beliefs. He has such a wonderful approach to his belief system. He's very spiritual, very dedicated, and yet his beliefs somehow embrace the whole world. He manages to display respect and find value in all points of view.

All in all, I found it to be a spiritually uplifting program. So one day I was attempting to share what I got from the program, the thoughts and feelings it inspired in me, with Caryn. Since this man is a Christian, I'm thinking, "here's a guy who's a Christian, a Methodist minister, he teaches religion at a university, I think she will appreciate this perspective."

Sometimes there are things that impress me, from a spiritual perspective, and otherwise, but I know it's not something she's interested in. Sometimes I have to try to curb my enthusiasm and natural inclination to share things I consider important with people I consider important because . . . well, I'm not exactly sure why . . . except to say they aren't where I am. Which is not the same as saying they are wrong. I guess you could say, "we get what we get when we're ready to get it." . . . Get it???

This man, Huston Smith was so well-spoken, brilliant, I thought. Bill Moyers asks such great questions and is one of my heros besides.

So I was seeing this as something that she would enjoy; a perspective I could share that she would appreciate, something that would enrich her life. I began discussing the program with her but I could see immediately when I started talking that she was withdrawing, mentally or spiritually. Or both. I don't remember exactly what we said but before that conversation was over, I felt as though she was feeling sad or threatened or something . . . unpleasant. I think I actually saw tears in her eyes.

And then I felt very bad. I hadn't planned to cause her any pain; certainly didn't want to hurt her feelings. I was trying to share something with her I thought she would find spiritually uplifting. But finally I realized it was having just the opposite effect.

After she went home, I tried to think this through to understand better and I thought why in the world, when I try to share these things with my children, who are dear to me, does it seem to have the wrong effect? A little voice inside, the Holy Spirit or my gut, or my psyche – who knows for sure what it was – but some little voice inside me said, "the problem is you think that you are bringing something additional to her and she's afraid that you're attempting to take something away."

And I realized, "well, that really is kind of the way it is. My intent was to share something that for me enriched my spiritual understanding but she reacted as though I was criticizing her belief system and then she felt threatened.

This really makes me sad. Because it is totally **not** what I'm trying to do. Recognizing that this is happening helps me understand I need to stop trying to share things of this nature with my children and some others. Others, for instance, like Julie and Judy. Our life experiences have been quite different since high school days. We likely do not have so much in common anymore and a late-night gab session might prove to be more uncomfortable than not.

Somehow on that night of our reunion, I had that sense of concern when I was with Judy and Julie. Concern that if we spent a lot of time together that night, we might get into some of those kinds of conversations. I suspected they might not think the same way as me and they might be hurt or angry or offended with my perspective. And I really had no intention of doing any of those things. All I really wished I could have done was basically just give them a hug and say, "my god, we made it this far, didn't we. Isn't that great!"

So, sensing this the night of our reunion, I never really embraced the opportunity that would have made such conversations possible. Still, I felt disappointed and saddened by this realization.

I would have loved to have talked to them about yukky menopause and ask how they got through it. I think I'm still in it and it's kind of a pain in the butt. Lots of things I would have liked to have talked to them about, too; raising kids, and men, and love, and . . . I'm sorry we didn't get to do that. Maybe next time . . .

I do think it's important to learn who you can talk to about what. I know I have friends at the Unitarian Church, and others, people I've met through the years, not relatives, and we can sit down and talk about who and what we are or what we think and there is some kind of easy comraderie there. No one of us seems to be threatened if another person doesn't exactly agree.

I go to meetings at the Unitarian Church where we discuss all sorts of things. There's really a wide assortment of people there. Because the people who go to this church have all sorts of beliefs. Some of them believe in God, some of them don't, some of them have Jewish backgrounds, some of them have Church of Christ backgrounds; they're all in different stages of belief. But still, there is a distinct atmosphere of respect and tolerance. In fact, Unitarians joke about themselves and say, "is it intolerant to be intolerant of intolerance?"

It is so refreshing to sit and discuss ideas where people contribute their points of view and it's like everybody thinks, oh, wow, that's neat, I never thought of it that way. Or maybe they don't think that way. But whatever they think, they don't find the other person's ideas threatening. And it's comfortable and accepting and such an easy kind of conversation.

I just wish I could have those kinds of conversations with the people I care most about. Sometimes Scott and I have these kinds of conversations. And I feel the same thing coming from him. That's why I don't like to get into discussions with him. It wasn't like that in our beginning. Now he just wants me to see his point of view and agree with his point of view. And even though I see his point of view, I don't always agree. But he can't let it go.

He has to keep the conversation going, as though he thinks, "well, if you understood what I was saying, you'd agree with me." Which isn't true.

Sometimes I do understand what he's saying, and I still don't agree. I don't mind that he doesn't agree with me, I just wish it was okay if I don't agree with him. I think that's important for people to get to that point. If I really care about you and if I really have respect for you. It's got to be okay that I don't think exactly like you. I'm not you, I haven't lived your life, I haven't had your experiences so why on earth would I think exactly the same way. (I thought we had figured this out a long time ago when we decided to be "best friends".)

Is this Rocket Science??? I don't think so.

Oh, well, now I'm rambling. But it bothers me that sometimes this happens with Scott and my children. I wish it wasn't so. Because if there's anybody I want to be loving with and have a good relationship with it's my children and my partner.

All in all, the trip was really a neat thing. I enjoyed seeing Nick.[12] Scott and I had lunch with him and went way over time. That's what made me late for the reunion. And now I'm writing about it here in my "journal". Plus I have to transcribe everything I taped the night of

---

[12] Long-term boyfriend from high school; see Teenage Romance – Fifties Style

the reunion to send to Jim Hoppin for the "memory book" he is going to prepare for everyone who attended.

When I type up all this stuff for Jim I'm going to put my little part in there and I'm just going to write a little essay called, The Reunion. Well, that's enough for today.

Goodbye.

* * * * *

Changed my mind. I'm going to talk some more because Scott and I were talking about some things on the way home and I think they're kind of interesting and I'd like to remember that I said them some time. Maybe I can use them somehow, some way, in something I write.

Mostly it's about the kind of person I am. I don't know why I'm like this. But all through my life there's been a part of me that stands off on the sidelines and watches what's going on. I don't know if that's what everybody does but I do it.

I do the same thing in my head. I have all these imaginary conversations with people. As a result of something I've seen on TV or maybe the last time I was with them we did this and that or just like with this reunion I sit here and I imagine, gee, I would have liked to have talked to Julie and Judy about blah, blah, blah, blah, blah.

Maybe everybody does that; I don't know.

So the point of what I'm trying to say right here is this – if can get this idea expressed. The thing that's frustrating to me is, I know that everybody, as we get older, realizes that life is very, very short, and it becomes more precious with each passing day. And all the things you thought were important when you were young really aren't important. What's important is listening to the birds – which I'm doing right now – I can hear them outside in my tree. I've got several big trees and I love it. The sun is shining, it's a beautiful fall day. And those are the kinds of things that I love.

Working in my garden, being with my family. Not conquering Corporate America. I have no interest in that whatsoever. It's a good thing because I never would have made it and I'd have been very disappointed. But, anyway, I'm trying to get to a point here.

WHICH IS:

Now that I'm older and now that time does seem to fly – life does seem so fleeting – it becomes ever more precious. And I am frustrated because – I am so aware of how precious it is and how fast it's going that I'm afraid I'm going to worry about it so much that I don't enjoy what's left.

To illustrate more clearly (I hope):

I've always been this kind of person when it comes to vacations. Whatever length of time my vacation is, say it's ten days or five days or two weeks, whatever. The day before the vacation ends, the day before I'm to go home, I lose that day of vacation because I spend all my time and energy thinking and organizing and getting ready to go home the next day. And what I'm thinking is, "Why on earth do I have to be that way?"

What I wish I could do is enjoy the next-to-last day as part of the vacation. I want to do vacation things. And then when the last day comes, the day to go home, that's soon enough to worry about going home.

Except it never works that way for me. Whatever day is the last day of vacation, the day for returning home, I'm going to miss the next-to-last day also.

So I worry that I'll do the same thing with my life. I'm so busy realizing and thinking about how precious it is and how short it is, it's like I'm in the second to the last day of the vacation (life) and I'm already worrying about the last day of the vacation (life).

I had a grandpa who, from the time he was 60 years old – Bless his dear heart, I loved him to death – acted old and talked about being old and to hear him talk you'd have thought he was going to die tomorrow. He did that for 30 years.

I don't want to be that way. And it's not a physical thing. It's a mental thing. For me. It might have been physical for him because maybe he didn't feel well, I don't know. But he lived to be NINETY-SEVEN!!

I do not want to be that way. I do not want to miss the next-to-last day of vacation/life. Maybe that's something I can learn how to do. But I think it's just the way I am.

And that IS the end of that.

October 1996

– REFLECTIONS –

I re-read Nick's lovely note and poem this morning. Then I re-read our story; the story I wrote about him and me when we were teenager lovers. And I cried.

His note came in the mail yesterday. I had finally decided that what he said when we met for lunch last month – that he never writes or sends cards anymore – was still true. And that the story I had written and given him about our teenage love affair was not going to change that pattern.

But I was wrong. He finally wrote a lovely note, accompanied by his reflections of our time together; a poem called, "Dawn[13] of my Youth."

I cried.

I cry easily these years . . . when I think of my parents . . . when I think of the difficulties my children are facing as they deal with being married, earning a living, and raising their families . . . when I think of all the little children and animals that are in pain or suffering.

And then I have to try to analyze my feelings. Sometimes I figure it out; sometimes I don't.

Actually, I think it's just my feelings about life that overflow my heart and spill out my eyes as tears. The good in life, the bad. The beauty, the joy, the pain. The Ying and Yang of it all. At this stage in my life, I've experienced more than less of it. Youth, young adulthood, being a wife, a mother, and now a grandmother. Hopefully, I will never have to face the death of a child. Death of parents is yet to come but their age of 84 brings it ever closer. I think I will not be able to bear it; yet somehow I know that I will.

With regard to my little story and the note Nick sent in reply, I think I'm crying for the innocence and youth of the two young people we were. From this distance of 58 years, I look back at them and I am overcome with emotion. I don't know why. I just feel love for them both. And in an instant of understanding realize I am wishing somehow I could have protected them from what life was going to do to them.

Not that life did such terrible things. Life taught them what it had to teach them. They became the Nick and Sarah of today.

From our short luncheon visit a few weeks ago, I got the impression the Nick of today has become someone I would like and could identify with. Not overly conservative politically or religiously.

So maybe we could relate pretty well as mature adults. Something in his manner or speech made me think he is sensitive to the spiritual side of life also. A pleasing observation, if accurate.

On the other hand, it has been over 30 years since we shared anything of ourselves and we might have little in common if the opportunity to find out ever presented itself. Which is not likely to happen.

I get frustrated when I experience these emotions. Whatever the source. I believe if I could put these feelings into words, I would be writing something important.

But it is hard to do.

Teenage Nick and Sarah had a long-term relationship (seven years) that provided a measure of security and stability which allowed them to practice and learn what love is all about.

Somewhere along the way of life – because I am a woman, and because I lived at the time that I lived, because I helped raise four children, because I had to make it on my own for a time – I became the person I am today.

Actually, I can finally say: I like this person I've become. She is the fulfillment of the potential of that young girl of so many years ago.

Sometimes it makes her sad and she cries because she never found the love, appreciation, and acceptance of who and what she thinks she is. Maybe she's deceiving herself? She has always wondered what is it that her childhood friend, Julie, managed to learn and understand about life and love and marriage that enabled her and her husband, Jim, to survive it all. Happily. And she is envious.

For herself, she has come to the conclusion there is no "kindred spirit".

Does this begin to sound like a pity party? I think so. I'm just going to write a little essay.

When I was married to Jerry, I bemoaned our relationship and engaged in a great deal of "if only" thinking. One example in particular sticks in my memory because I thought it often.

I once heard someone compare a woman to a sensitive, high-spirited, finely-trained thoroughbred race horse. At the time I thought the analogy fit.

"If only Jerry could understand I am like that thoroughbred horse. He uses such a heavy hand on me. As though I were a field work horse. I'm not. His heavy-handed treatment is breaking me. If he would use a lighter touch he would realize how readily I would respond and perform. In ways that would surpass his expectations."

Yuk! How ignorant this sounds now. As though I were his property!

Twenty-five years later along comes Scott. And I think I've found my knight in shining armor. My feelings for him reminded me of falling in love with Nick. I felt like a teenager again. Scott was youthful and full of fun. He liked to do things on the spur of the moment. He had a motorcycle. We rode it all over Nashville and "surrounds". He claimed to be a feminist and said he liked independent women. He also was skeptical of love and did not believe it lasted.

I poured out my love. I saw him as a needy child who had never learned that love is unconditional. It lasts. No matter what.

So I loved and nurtured him. As long as I could. I knew he would come to realize and appreciate what I was offering. The protective barriers he had erected would be torn down. After he had received this unconditional love long enough, he would learn to appreciate it and give it in return. Wrong.

By the time he finally asked me to marry him in early 1991, I had come to the disappointing conclusion our relationship would never culminate in marriage. Whatever had happened to Scott to bring him to singlehood as a way of life was too ingrained to be changed. I had always determined I would never be the one to bring up the subject of marriage. And I hadn't. I would give all I had to give and wait for the realization of what he had to dawn on him. If it didn't, then we both would be the losers.

So by the time he finally asked me to marry him I had become convinced of the fact that it wasn't going to happen and it would be in my best interests to leave. If I had been younger, I would have. But I had gotten very comfortable and relatively safe in this relationship. Just sharing living expenses was a big consideration at this stage in my life. I had come to believe that Scott loved me as much as he could love anybody. But the "light bulb" had never gone off in his brain like I had hoped. My knight in shining armor had never come to the realization – "Oh, my god, this is the woman of my dreams! How lucky I am to have found her at last."

Just as I had used the metaphor of a thoroughbred race horse for myself in the context of my first marriage, I now compared myself to a rose.

A rose is a thing of beauty. But it needs special care. It is susceptible to all sorts of diseases. AND it has tiny little thorns that can prick you and hurt you – even draw blood – if you're not careful.

I wanted Scott to see me as a rose. And treasure me. And show me the care a rose needs. Instead, he let me wither on the vine. Now sometimes when he passes by or tries to touch me, he gets pricked by the thorns.

My own needs have been too long neglected. In the long run, I guess we all are selfish characters. I gave and gave and thought eventually I would get in return. But I didn't. Little by little, I stopped giving.

Is it selfishness or self-preservation?

Now all I want is peace and quiet. Time to work on the things I need and like to work on – my writing, my home-based secretarial business (because we need the money but it's not enough), the yard, visiting with friends and children.

Forget sex. Scott always made me feel self-conscious about my body even in our early times when I weighed 97 pounds. I never ran around naked, though I would have liked to, because I didn't want to expose my flaws to his detailed scrutiny. Now that I weigh 20 pounds more than I ever have in my life, I'd never show him my body. Plus he never wants to do it anyway.

In fairness, I guess men his age worry about heart attacks from the exertion. I can understand that. But I don't think he's even suggested having intercourse -- in any way -- in at least two years. I just "take care" of him from time to time. In the way that I know and do so well. And that he enjoys so much.

That's okay I guess. If you don't feel loved and appreciated, something happens to your own sexual feelings. They just go away. At my age, most of the time I just don't care anymore.

Getting Nick's note and rereading the story I wrote about us once more rekindled the need and wish universal to the human heart to be cherished and loved.

When I stopped crying, I penned a note to Nick.

11/5/96

Dear Nick –

Sitting here at my dining room table with my morning coffee thinking of what I wanted to say in my brief note of thanks, WAMB started playing "SH-BOOM" and a grin coursed through my body.

Immediately into the camera of my mind came the picture of us on a Saturday afternoon driving (in the "leaded in" 1950 black Ford with white "skirts") to a church baseball game with this song on the radio and us singing along at the top of our lungs!

The innocence, the joy of those youthful times. I wish everyone had such memories to look back on. My childhood and teenage years make me wish society could return to those safe, respectful times. Even though I know those same times were not so wonderful for others in our society. Still, for us, they were, weren't they?

So – I guess you liked the story.

Thank you for the poem. I will add it to my box of cherished things of my life; a lovely, thoughtful addition.

Godspeed, dear friend –

Sarah

Dawn(*) of my Youth

What sweet, sweet remembrances
of a life so long ago,
no doubt your warm forgiving ways
are why I loved you so.

A friend, it's said,
sifts through the wheat
and casts all chaff aside,
preferring to forget the flaws
that time and truth can't hide.

We learned to love,
to give, to take,
and when our time was through,
I tried to give to other souls
the things I learned with you.

We cannot know
(its not revealed)
the things we might have done,
But no one could dispel those dreams
when our two hearts were one.

So . . .
Forever and ever,
my heart will be true:
As the sweetheart of my youth,
I'll remember you.

Nick Dalton
October 1996

(*) My real name; using "Sarah" here would destroy the meaning of the title and poem. Also, unknown to you, dear reader, is the significance of the first two lines of the last stanza. It is from a song that was popular when we were dating. And which he had penned to me in a letter one of the summers of our love when we were apart and missing each other.

SARAH'S STORY

Merry Christmas and Happy New Year from Sarah and Scott Jensen

December 23, 1996

Aaah, the Christmas countdown has arrived. All the shopping, cleaning, wrapping, and baking is done. Nothing left to do but enjoy. Right? Well, I hope that's true for you, anyway, even though I can't claim that accomplishment. Nonetheless, I know it will eventually come together. As soon as I get the cleaning, the wrapping, and the baking done!

The Tennessee portion of the clan will be here for dinner, of course. That means Caryn and Randy (though he works Christmas Day till 10 p.m. at Opryland), John, Kim, and Jeremy, Scott's dad and brother, Mike, plus two close friends who don't have family nearby. And our renter, Jay, who also is alone.

Sometime during this two-week period, I'll drive over to Jackson with whichever kids are available and have a little bit of Christmas celebration with my folks. My mom has become so sweet and childlike in her appreciations, it is delightful and heartbreaking both. I understand there's been a breakthrough of sorts with women Alzheimer patients by putting them on ERT. I contacted my mother's doctor and he agreed to suggest it at her next visit in January. Thanks to the tip from Connie (West) I also asked him to consider vitamin B-12 supplements. My dad, of course, continues to stay interested in and busy with his movie/computer programs. I think he may achieve sainthood soon, as well.

Tom and Josie and Lisa and Mo(*) will have the usual Sullivan extravaganza in Michigan, which has become Christmas Eve at Jerry and Nancy's and Christmas Day at Linda and Ray's. Even the crumbs from those meals will be scrumptious, I know.

Tom and Josie and troop came down in May. John, Kim, Jeremy, me, and them plus tons of camping gear all went to Fall Creek Falls and spent a soggy, wet, wonderful weekend together (Scott was still over-the-road). Tom and family came back down at Thanksgiving. As did Jerry and Nancy, and their best friends, Ruth and Chuck. They all had Thanksgiving Day dinner together at O'Charley's, we all met at Caryn and Randy's to celebrate Josie's birthday later that evening, and then the kids came to our house the next day for a second holiday dinner.

Speaking of Caryn and Randy, they bought their first house a couple of months ago. It's small but it's theirs and they are thrilled. Their black cat had kittens two weeks prior to moving so we now have our third – and last – cat, too. He was the littlest one and is all black like his mother. He was born just before Halloween so we call him CD (short for Count Dracula). For a cat, he is adorable. We have new next-door neighbors now, however, and a female boxer with pups moved in about the same time we got the kitty. She has attracted many other large dogs so kitty stays inside except for scheduled outings with me.

We made a quick trip to Michigan in late September for my 40th high school reunion. One of our classmates (sometimes perceived as the least likely to succeed – I love it!!!) has a fleet of three river boats for cruising the Detroit River and we met on one for a wonderful dinner and night of reminiscing. I had heard the 40th would be the best, and it was. All the posturing, etc. is over and we all felt free to express affection for each other and the fact that we've made it this far. It was great! The evening was especially memorable for me and prompted me to write another essay, "The Reunion," in which I preserve the experience.

Scott and I had met with Nick Dalton for a late lunch Saturday afternoon prior to the party. It was wonderful seeing him. I just wish we could have had more time to reminisce and find out who we've become. As it was, we stayed longer than planned. So what happened later that evening is partly his fault (or should I say the resulting story is partly to his credit.).

I volunteered to help put a memory booklet together to commemorate the evening. I took my tape recorder. Everyone spoke to me personally or I taped their comments at the microphone after dinner when they told us what they'd been doing for the last 40 years. When we returned to Tennessee, I typed up everyone's comments and mailed out copies for them to correct, change, whatever. When I got the comments back, I sent the packet to another classmate (sometimes perceived as one of the most likely to succeed – and he did!!) who is putting it all together. Don't know if he'll include my essay in the booklet or not but it really doesn't matter. I got a kick out of writing it anyway. And it will eventually become part of my book, Letters and Essays of An Ordinary Woman, (or something like that).

Workwise, I continue my slave labor deposition work.

Some time ago, I made contact with a would-be writer on AOL who was looking for a ghost writer. He sent me the first 40 pages of his manuscript, I rewrote his first 12 pages, which became 40 pages consisting of a prologue and four chapters, which became the proposal. He is supposed to be sending it out but he gets discouraged easily, is intimidated by his computer, and needs me to hand-hold him through the process. I can't do that. He has a worthwhile story to tell, which is a true story about corruption and whistle-blowing in the juvenile justice system (he's the whistle-blower) but he's not a writer, I don't know if I'm a good enough writer, and it is very difficult to get published anyway. So don't know if anything will ever come of this project.

In my spare time, I write. I now have had three (!!!) articles published and am collaborating on a fourth with a writer from Mason, Michigan, that I met when I was covering the Columbia Mule Days Festival back in April. (I wrote 3000 words for Rural Heritage – they published two paragraphs!!) Since this latest project is an assignment from the editor, I'm sure it will be published. I recently learned you only need 3 articles to get listed in The Literary Marketplace, which is the bible for people looking for ghost writers. Once we finalize this last article, I plan to contact them to get listed. Then sit back and wait while the writing assignments pour in. HA!

Additionally, another colleague has given me the name of a publisher who needs copy editors to work at home with their computers. She said they especially need people with legal backgrounds and thinks my work with court reporters and lawyers will be a plus if I contact them.

So those two things will be priorities right after the holidays.

Some of the best news of all is in early September Scott answered an ad for a teaching position at Nashville Tech and they hired him! He is teaching their truck driving course. During the past eight years of driving, he's logged three years over-the-road and been to all 48 contiguous states plus Canada. That plus his degrees and teaching experience made him the ideal man for the job, I reckon.

Needless to say, he is delighted to have a life once more and grateful to be "following his bliss". The person who preceded him "taught" from a hand-written 8-1/2 x 11 piece of paper on which he had written topics to discuss. Mostly he put the students directly into the trucks. Needless to say, Scott has immersed himself in procuring textbooks, developing lesson plans, contacting industry reps, etc. He held his first advisory committee meeting last week and everyone, including the director of the school, seemed impressed with what has been accomplished and what is planned. Of course I am thrilled and happy to see him pursuing his true vocation once again.

All in all, it's been a good year. A little older and hopefully wiser as we learn to make the most of now. For myself, I'm learning I don't have time for negatives anymore. It has become important to me to concentrate on and look for the goodness, the beauty, the kindness, the love. I know I don't always project this myself – that's the hard part – but I'm tryin'.

May the peace and joy of the holiday season be yours the whole year through.

Love,
Sarah

(*)Lisa is back in Michigan and her significant others – like musical chairs – come and go. As in, Steve is gone, Mo is back.

Summer 1997

– Life Force –

The slender young Vietnamese girl stood with her arms around the neck of the tall, blond American GI. The traditional pants and tunic of the girl's cultural attire coupled with the boy's Army fatigues only accented their youthful bodies. Yet they weren't dressed provocatively. The play was "Miss Saigon" and we knew it would not have a happy ending.

Scene upon scene produced the intended result as the audience was drawn into the emotions of the drama unfolding on stage. The characters acting out their tragic story took us with them as we too were caught up in the emotions being portrayed before us.

As I watched the young lovers move and sing and talk to each other, a cry of terrible anguish deep inside my gut began its silent journey through my psyche. Simultaneously, my heart sang with joy watching the awesome beauty of youthful love being expressed before me. The pervasive passion that erupts when young body embraces young body.

The pain in my gut was visceral and intense knowing I am past that time in life. No longer young. No longer slender. Most of the time that is okay and I am content.

Tonight I am not.

Love between the sexes is not limited to the young, of course. But it is, I think, **in spite of** the realities of time. Not the result of.

I was young and slender and pretty. . . just yesterday I think it was. The men of my youth were young and strong and expressed their love to me in much the same way as the young man on stage tonight was doing.

It went by so fast! Did I not see how beautiful it was until now?

* * * * *

I leave the theater with a heightened sense of what it means to be a woman who has loved this way. Filled once more with the sense of mystery of what it is that makes a man a man. They fight our wars and subdue our bodies. We are both repelled and enticed by the strength and courage and emotion that produces these acts.

Sitting here at my computer attempting to put my feelings into words, I am grateful to the gods for this glorious gift bestowed upon humanity, this life force attraction between the sexes. Seeing it characterized in plays and stories and in the lives of young people around me stir my own memories and renews in me a sense of awe for the beauty that is mankind.

Journal Entry, 08/03/97

Recovering from this severe back injury, on blood pressure medication for the first time, plus other pain and muscle relaxants, experiencing anew a couple of "panic attacks" or hypoglycemic attacks – or something – coffee withdrawal, Lorazepam, who knows – I sit listening to my Praise tape.

Often, I have noticed that while my intent is to immerse myself in the music and the praise, my mind wanders. Many times I get insight and/or ideas for things to write about.

Today is no exception –

- the playpen concept–a child's need for security/structure, to "protect him from himself"
- wondering how I've managed to screw up my life – and that of my children – so badly
- why did my learning to be a strong woman apparently have to destroy the love of two men?

Reflecting on the events that have occurred in my life since that fateful day in 1982 when Jerry finally announced he was, in fact, returning to Michigan, alone, I find myself thinking

- if I could go back to that day –
- or change all that I did prior to bring that day about –

I would get down on my hands and knees and beg and promise whatever I had to, to keep him from going – or leaving without the rest of us.

I never thought I would come to such a conclusion.

Long ago I had come to believe that Jerry and I were just too different to be able to make it. That, in the long run, the break-up was inevitable. Wondering why my developing confidence, self-esteem, and strength had to be at the expense of my marriage. Deciding that strong men are not threatened by strong women – i.e., Jerry was not a strong man.

I still feel that way and believe the same dynamics have resulted in the destruction of this second and final romantic relationship, as well.

Assuming I am correct, why must it be this way?

Or am I the crazy one? Am I really so ignorant of what loving someone is all about?

I thought I knew by the time Scott and I met.

I saw a little boy who had a traumatic childhood, mentally and physically abused, learning to protect himself by holding in and not expressing his feelings. But if I loved him long enough and good enough and hard enough, the armor around his emotions would crack and he would give back to me what I had so freely given to him.

It never happened.

Being only human myself, I was unable to keep up that level of love and nurturing without getting something in return.

I've always felt having to make it on my own after Jerry left – being a single mom trying to raise my children – made me stronger. Adversity, afterall, does make you or break you.

Now, because of financial and health concerns, however, I find myself wondering if it has been worth this. This being if I can't be healthy enough to work, how shall I survive?

So I find myself thinking –

Where would I be, where would we all be, if we could somehow go back and reverse the outcome, return our whole family to Michigan and start over. Reverse the decision that moved us to Tennessee.

At least financially, I would be safe.

Health-wise, I don't know. Life with Jerry had been stressful. Life beyond Jerry has been very different but equally stressful. So maybe the cost to my body would have been the same.

Right now, the price I've paid for the choice I've made seems very high and I wonder what the price for staying would have been? The cost of my health? My soul as a woman?

All I know is, it is frightening to be 59 years old, unsure of your health and ability to earn an income, and be dependent on someone (Scott) who is only willing and barely able to financially and emotionally take care of one person – himself.

December 17, 1997

Dear Wayne –

I ***did*** get your card and letter before sending mine. Actually, I decided to skip the Christmas letter crap this year. But did want to respond to your hand-written note. It is so thoughtful of you to always add your own personal note to your card each year.

For me, it gets harder each year to generate the necessary enthusiasm for the holidays. The responsibility for making this a special time just isn't shared. Some people just shouldn't be homeowners, you know?

A year ago last summer, while Scott was still over-the-road with Marine Cross Country delivering boats, I painted the entire house inside – except for the ceilings and one bedroom. Which means living/dining room, kitchen, den (actually a middle bedroom that we turned into an office/den), bath, one bedroom, and hall (with EIGHT doors; i.e., woodwork!!!!!) WITH A BRUSH!!! (I could only do about one wall at a time and it was more trouble than it was worth to use a pan and roller.)

That hall could probably go in the Guinness Book of Records as the smallest hall with the most doorways!

I used taupe (mouse color) on the walls and white on the woodwork in LR/DR, den, and hall. Everyone says the colors are beautiful. I think so too. Then I took up the carpet in the living/dining room and den. The living/dining room now has matching oriental rugs on hardwood floors. So does the den. But the ceilings are still atrocious!!!

Every room has odds and ends of things that need to be finished. Don't even ask about the kitchen. I painted the walls colonial blue with white woodwork. I had hoped to put red brick tile on the floor but we can't really afford to do anything else. (The walls had been yucky yellow with Halloween orange cupboards! I lived with that for TEN YEARS!)

John's buddy, who is in the cabinet building/home remodeling business built and installed a much needed cabinet that extends out into the kitchen from the wall and has a lowered side counter for eating. It still hasn't been painted. Plus the wall behind it has to be repainted because we pulled off the butcher board shelf that originally hung there and used it as the eating counter on the cabinet.

Unless I play Mother, nothing gets done. And I'm tired of playing Mother. So I think I'll just pass on the decorating this year too. We've never had room for a tree so decorating is just sitting things around on tables anyway.

The kids go to Michigan each year they can and this is one of those years. I'm so glad for them whenever they can share in that wonderful on-going family holiday tradition up there in the hinterland. But with them gone, it means I don't have to cook and clean and fuss if I don't want. And right now, I don't want. Whenever they go to Michigan for Christmas, we try and get together on New Year's Eve for snacks and stuff.

Why did you say, "give me a note and tell me more about. . ." You should know better by now.

To continue. You asked about my parents. I dread the phone call I know could come at any time. I'm enclosing an essay I wrote called "The Visit". I'm in the processing of revising it but it will address your inquiry about them.

Emotionally, my mother getting Alzheimer's is the worst thing I've experienced in my life so far. And I know it's **her** life, not mine. But it breaks **my** heart.

I guess we always think we're special. We don't **think** we think it until something like this happens. And then when we actually come face to face with something as awful as Alzheimer's, for instance, we realize that instead of saying, why me/us, the question really is, why not me/us. Does this make sense?

So far in my life, whatever has happened, eventually I have been able to say, well, I can deal with that. That's not so bad. It could be worse. So far, though, this is the worst. I try to imagine what it must be like to have these spots that just go dead in your brain, places where the light just clicks off from time to time. Oftener and oftener. It must be very confusing and frightening.

Every time I visit, I sit with her for a few minutes before I go. She cries and I cry. In her crying what I hear is that she knows something is very, very wrong with her and it makes her very, very sad. I hear her crying for the ways things used to be and for the way things are now. And I cry too.

With regard to the enclosure. Most of my writing has a major fault. I TELL instead of SHOW. I know I do it. It's easier. But not as readable/publishable. So starting with this essay I'm going to try and rewrite most of them with more dialogue and less narrative. Turn them into stories instead of essays. And give my characters fictitious names.

Regarding the old gang. You stay in touch much better than me.

As I mentioned in last year's letter, we saw Ruth and Chuck (and Jerry and Nancy) when they came to Tennessee last Thanksgiving. We all met at Randy and Caryn's house to celebrate Josie's birthday.

I had invited Ruth and Chuck to have dinner with us the night before but they called and canceled at the last minute. (?) Chuck called actually. And said they weren't up to it. I thought that was strange. I was very disappointed. I'd been looking forward to a good old-fashioned gab session with Ruth. We talked briefly at Caryn's but I felt very distant from her. I guess the years are really hard to bridge after all.

I really enjoyed our lunch with Nick (the weekend we went to Michigan for my reunion). Nick complimented me on not looking my age. Which, of course, put a smile in my soul. I gave him a copy of my story about our teenage romance. A few weeks later he sent me a poem he wrote about our relationship. It was lovely and I added it to my pile of treasured mementos.

Regarding children. I love the picture you enclose with your card each year. I always cry for a minute when I look at it. I'm not sure why. Just thinking about old times, I guess. And realizing how many years have passed since those times. And how we all have changed. Your "daughters" are lovely. How great to have a relative living overseas to visit!

My brood is doing reasonably well although Lisa continues to have a very hard time. From where I sit it seems she should be getting more support and less criticism from her dad than she does. But then what do I know. That's the way he's been to each of us (me and the kids, that is) at one time or another. I don't mean for that to sound acrimonious though it probably does.

Each one of my kids seems to me to be the most wonderful child that ever walked the face of this earth. It hurts me that I don't have the resources to be more helpful to them, especially Lisa. Maybe in the long run it's a blessing.

My brother just moved back with my folks temporarily (it's driving them all more crazy than they already are). Just prior to the move, I was talking with my dad and he said, "well, your kids are always your kids. And they can always come home if they need to."

I don't feel I have the option to say that to my children and it hurts. Another legacy of divorce and remarriage. At least this one.

It sounds like you're comfortable with your church affiliation at last. I'm so glad for you. You seemed rather distraught over that a few letters ago. (Do you remember?) But then just about anything would be an improvement over the way we were raised, don't you think? And it sounds like you've finally severed the cord. And that's got to be good. Right?

Now, about me and Scott –

Things just don't seem to work out the way you expect sometimes, you know? The events of this past summer will illustrate what I mean, I think.

We planned an 11-day vacation/writing research trip. We left on June 28th and spent the first night in Natchez, Mississippi. It was delightful. Spent most of the next day touring the city, especially visiting all the old mansions there.

Late the next afternoon we headed on to Lafayette, Louisiana, to visit Scott's daughter, Bonnie. She and her husband moved there a few months ago when he accepted a position with an oil rigging company. Bonnie had been working full-time in St. Louis and Jake was getting his master's in geological engineering (or something like that) when this company made him an offer he couldn't refuse. Sixty thou to start!!!!! Twenty-four years old!!!!! So they went!

We got to their condo (Jake was out of town) Friday evening. Saturday morning Bonnie drove us to New Orleans and we did the Bourbon Street tourist thing. Neither Scott or I had ever been. It was great fun!

Bonnie drove. It took 2-1/2 hours each way. Plus 7-8 hours of walking and touristing in the city. We also went to that famous graveyard where Marie Leveaux is buried. Bonnie had a small car (Nissan, I think). I wanted Scott and Bonnie to have the chance to visit as much as possible so I sat in the back. Going and coming. When I tried to get out of the car at eleven o'clock that night, I couldn't stand up straight.

No big deal, I thought. I slept on the couch with my legs up all night. Wasn't any better the next morning. Bought some Aleve and spent the day sightseeing around Lafayette with Bonnie. Monday we drove on to Houston where Scott had a Tuesday morning meeting with a director of a school similar to his. Left Houston heading back to Louisiana and more sightseeing. (We wanted to take as many back roads and see as many small towns and old characters in them as possible; i.e., the writing research part).

SARAH'S STORY

Sitting riding in the car didn't hurt too much. Getting out and trying to walk did. Thirty miles or so this side of Little Rock, Arkansas, I finally told Scott I didn't think I could go any further. He had offered to drive us straight through to Nashville but since we had planned to spend the last three days of the trip in Malden, Missouri, where all his old buddies live plus his high school reunion was planned for the 4th of July, I told him to go on with the trip alone and I would fly home from Little Rock. (Me who hates to fly!)

When we got to the airport, we called Caryn's house and talked to Randy and asked if one of them could pick me up at the Nashville airport. We told him Scott would call back after we found out what flight I would be arriving on. We got my ticket (they put me in a wheelchair at the airport) with ten minutes to spare. They put me on the plane and we took off.

When I got to Nashville, they put me in a wheelchair again. I waited at my gate for Caryn or Randy to appear. No one came. I had them paged. After 20 minutes, I finally called their house. They were in bed asleep. Scott had never called! Caryn jumped out of bed and came and got me.

Scott called me from Malden the next day. I asked him why he hadn't called Caryn to tell her when my flight would arrive. He said, "Oh, I forgot."

The upshot to me physically from all this was I went to the emergency room three times, once by ambulance. The third time they took an MRI which showed I had a herniated disc at L4-5. That time I stayed three days. They gave me an epidural (cortisone injection in the spine) the next day and sent me home the next day after that.

Eventually I had two more epidurals as an out-patient. The spine specialist who put me in the hospital said he expected I would eventually ask to have the "operation". I was flat on my stomach on a pallet on the living room floor for 2-1/2 months. I would get up to eat, go to the bathroom, and walk for 10 minutes at a time on my little front walk.

Slowly but surely I have improved. Not being able to drive was the pits. I finally started that again in September. By October I began to resume my usual activities, including mowing the lawn. That and digging in the dirt (planting flowers, digging weeds) is what I missed most, I think. Right in the middle of all this, I called my dad and found out he was in the hospital with a broken leg! His second. (The first was in 1992.) Not being able to go and help them nearly broke my heart!

Physically this has been the most difficult thing that's ever happened to me. But I am finally nearly good as new. My back and leg still hurt but well within bearable limits. **Without** the operation.

A few months ago I read a book called, "The Passive/Aggressive Man". It fits Scott to a T. One of the things passive/aggressive men do is they "forget" things. Especially where their partner is concerned. It's the passive aspect of their aggression. Which they are afraid to express. Forgetting to call Caryn with my flight arrival time is just one of a succession of things forgotten in the past year or so. I liken it to an epiphany of understanding for me, however. Like when you get hit with the 2 x 4 board and say, "Oh, **now** I get it.

Oh, yes. I'm in the book too. Women who hook up with these men fall into various categories. One is "Manager", another is "Rescuer", another is "Mother". I've been a little bit of all of these at one stage of this relationship or another. Now I'm just tired.

But let me continue. And tell you about cats. It's relevant.

You have a couple so you know about cats. We have our third, and last, cat. He is Caryn's cat's baby. He is black. He thinks I'm his mother. In the way that cats love, he loves me very much. Which isn't exactly saying a whole lot. But then, he's a cat. And as a cat, he's delightful and I love him.

Actually, I'll just enclose the essay I wrote about the subject.

There's a line from the song "Desperado" that pretty much sums it up. It goes something like this: "A lot of fine things have been laid upon your table. But you only want the things that you can't have."

I think that describes Scott to a T.

I gave him all the nurturing, love, devotion, respect, admiration I had to give. I spread a banquet on his table. He took what he wanted, he ate his fill. He never seemed to notice what kind of food it was, whether there were flowers on the table or not, what kind of silverware was used. Never said please, thank you, give me more, give me less, nothing. Just took. Oh, he never complained, either.

Now all that's left of the banquet are scraps.

And you know what the saddest thing of all is? He doesn't have a clue as to how or why this happened.

He is a reasonably decent, good person. He isn't intentionally mean-spirited. As long as I don't question anything he does or ask for any help or disagree with any point of view he has, we live a peaceful, quiet, amiable life.

There now. Aren't you sorry you asked?

You asked about Julie and Jim Craig. So let me first tell you a little more about the reunion. It relates.

I spent most of the evening of the reunion talking with as many classmates as I could; taping their comments on my tape recorder. For the booklet Jim Hoppin was going to put together (which I've yet to see). I think I told you about that in last year's Christmas letter. As a result, I never did get a chance to sit down with Julie and Judy, the closest friends I'd had in high school. The strange thing is I had this funny feeling in my gut that talking with them would be difficult. Isn't that silly?

But not really.

I'd spoken to Julie a couple of times on the phone discussing our plans to get together during our reunion weekend and she'd made a point of telling me her nickname was "Mrs. Conservative".

During one phone conversation she brought me up to date on Judy's life too. She told me that Hugh had died a couple of years ago. Which I knew. I believe she said they had lost their business a few years prior to him getting sick. Or maybe his worry over the business is what made him sick. I'm not sure. What I remember from the conversation is that he had a chemical engineering firm and the government just about closed him down with all their environmental regulations.

As a result of the ensuing financial problems, Hugh's medical expenses, etc., I believe she said they lost their home. So now, instead of two, she only has the one home her parents gave them years ago. And now Judy has to work. I think Julie told me she was working at a school. Doing what, I don't know.

Julie sounded very indignant about all this and seemed to be blaming the government for most of Judy's troubles. I am certainly sorry for the difficulties Judy and Hugh encountered and for his untimely death. Losing a loving mate of many years would be traumatic. On the other hand, as you can probably guess, I tend to side with the environmentalists when it comes to their point of view versus that of big corporations. And as far as having to work, that's what most folks have to do.

As she talked, I realized my life and theirs had taken very different turns and I wondered if time and events had created a distance between us that would make a visit difficult or awkward.

So the night of the party I think I was subconsciously avoiding the opportunity of sitting down to really talk with the two of them. Part of me wanted to be with them but I had this gut feeling that either we'd have nothing in common to talk about or that I might say something to offend them. You know me, I'm inclined to view things from a liberal point of view.

So what happened was, when the party was over Judy offered to drive me back to Royal Oak (where Tom and Josie live and where we were staying). So we could finally have our visit. Which was so sweet and thoughtful of her.

Once we got in the car, they both asked me question after question about my kids, Scott, my folks, Nick, et cetera. And you know me, I talked and talked and talked. Every once in a while I asked them a question too but mostly I just answered their questions. It's just that I tend to give lengthy answers. Like my lengthy letters.

Then I made a really big mistake. I asked Julie a question and I think it really offended her. For good. (I haven't heard from her since. Even though I sent her a copy of her comments from the reunion to edit and return for the booklet).

I said something like, "Julie, I've just got to ask you this. It's something I've wondered about all these years. You know when you and Wayne and Nick and I were best friends and going steady? When we all were **"In Love?"**. Well, Nick and I always used to wonder about this. We were "doing it", you see. And we always wondered if you and Wayne were "doing it" too. So what I want to know is, did you?

There was this real long pause. And I realized I'd made a terrible faux pas.

(It was so long ago. I've even written about it. I'm no longer embarrassed or ashamed of what we did. In fact, just the opposite. It's provided me with some delightful memories of youthful indiscretions. Obtusely, it never occurred to me anyone else would feel uncomfortable or embarrassed about their teenage conduct either.)

Finally, after what seemed like ages of silence, she replied "no."

By now we were nearly back to my son's house. I don't remember the rest of the conversation. All I know is I felt embarrassed and angry with myself for making my best school chum uncomfortable by asking my stupid question. And I've not heard from her again. And that makes me sad.

All this is not by way of asking you the same question, by the way. I learned my lesson. It's still none of my business.

So that's what I know about Julie. I assume they're still in Texas. She told me Jim had been planning to retire soon but Three M had made him an offer he almost couldn't refuse and he was thinking of staying on another year or two.

They are very involved in their church as lay ministers. When he does finally retire, I believe they plan to work full time in the ministry. (Ain't life funny – Julie and Jim have become the fanatics and I've become the backslider. Except I don't consider myself to be a backslider at all. Just have a different way of looking at things now than then. And I don't really think they're fanatics. Dedicated. That's a better word.)

Because of my back injury, I pretty much had to give up my deposition work. It was extremely labor intensive anyway. Typing so many hours every day made my hands hurt. Probably arthritis. I have continued my writing, however, and am working on several essays about my parents, the enclosure being one of them.

Scott has been worried about our financial situation for some time now so about a month ago I took a part-time job. I work four hours a day at Cumberland Heights, which may increase to five or six hours per day. I hope I can hold it to five. They just created the job and there's too much work for four hours. I work at their outpatient alcohol/drug abuse rehabilitation clinic.

They have beautiful in-house facilities located out in the country at what they aptly call The Farm. The pay is atrocious but I'm enjoying the work anyway. I work for the DUI and Domestic Violence Program Coordinator. I didn't know if I'd be able to drive back and forth to a job and sit regularly in an office every day but it hasn't hurt me. In fact, I think I feel better with the additional activity.

Caryn and I get together once a week or so for dinner and a movie or errands or something and she recently told me, "Mom, there's a spark about you that was missing when you were just working at home." I feel that spark myself.

I have so many things I want to write about. People I want to interview. And whether I ever get it finished and/or published or not, my book is taking shape. I know what I want it to say. Much of it has already been said. In letters and ruminations through the years. It's just the putting it together that is time consuming and, at times, heart-wrenching.

Mostly I just take things one day at a time. After being flat on my back for so long, I promised myself I would never complain about running errands, getting groceries, gas, etc. again. So far I haven't. It's still wonderful to be able to get in my car and go wherever I have to go and do whatever I have to do.

And when Spring comes, I get to work in the yard again. Life is good.

* * * * *

I just reread my letter. And realized there's no way I can send this. All he did was ask, "so, how're things?" I can't saddle him with this soul-baring saga.

But it'll make a great chapter in my book.

Cats Are Good . . . Pets
(Written 10/26/96)

Scott loves cats. This is a good pet for him, I think. A cat is independent, pretty self-sufficient, doesn't need or want much from his humans. We have a cat. The occasional touch or pat from Scott or me is really all he needs. Wives are not cats, though.

Scott is a lot like a cat, I think

He never looks up from what he's doing if you come into the room; for instance, in the morning. I used to always greet him with a hug and kiss each morning or whenever he returned home. He never did it. I don't do it anymore.

He doesn't express appreciation for things that are done for him; food prepared, clothes washed, programs taped that he likes, typing of his ideas for books and stuff for his class. As many programs as I've taped for him, is it unreasonable of me to wonder why he never thinks to tape any for me? Often I'm still at my computer at 8 and 9 o'clock in the evening. If I were the one sitting watching TV and he was the one typing, it would be second nature for me to tape – or ask if he wanted me to tape – the programs I was watching.

I used to regularly fix his food on a plate and bring it to him. Always brought him coffee when I fixed mine. Whatever he might have been thinking about it, I don't know. What he said was nothing. It was as though he didn't notice – or took it as his due. He took the food, he ate it. He took the coffee, he drank it. Whatever is offered, he takes. No questions asked. No thanks expressed. On the other hand, he never complains either. That's something, I guess.

* * * * *

As Sarah explored it further, the analogy was quite fitting. For instance, their cat thought she was his mother. In the way that cats love, he loved her with every fiber of his being. Which isn't exactly saying a whole lot. But then he's a cat. And as a cat, he was delightful and she loved and accepted him in return.

Accepted the fact that, being a cat, he lived in the now. She didn't expect him to plan ahead or think about the past. The fact that he was totally self-absorbed and self-serving didn't bother her at all. He was a cat. Pretty much self-sufficient; a plus. In a cat.

Of course, cat-like, he also took whatever it was you had to give and then went on about his business. And when he looked at you, it was as though he looked right through you. He stared intently but you felt no connection. As opposed, for instance, to a dog, who when he looks at you, you think you can see his soul. Or at least his love and devotion.

Having now lived with Scott for ten years, six of those as man and wife, she realized how appropriate it was to compare his ability to participate in and maintain a personal relationship with that of a cat. Which is another way of saying some folks just shouldn't be married, you know?

*****

Scott doesn't have a mean bone in his body. He would never intentionally hurt any person, plant, or animal. He is without guile. He is intelligent. He is a reader and knows how to solve things "according to the book". But he is rigid in his thinking. By that I mean if things are not the way he expected them to be, he doesn't seem to know how to readjust his thinking – to look at a problem from a different perspective and find a solution. If the real life situation -- under the hood of the car, for instance – is different than the book, he is stumped. He is good-natured, but he is also a pessimist. He has a reverence for the earth and all its inhabitants and he worries about the future of the planet. He is a good man.

*****

Now I feel badly that I've said all this. Even though I believe it to be true.

Spring 1998

– THE RING –

Returning from work, she headed to her bedroom to change clothes. At the bedroom door, she stopped, momentarily stunned to see a pile of clothing on her bed as well as the plastic container where she kept her pantihose.

Because of her limited dresser space, these items – until now – had been stored in Scott's large chifferobe in his bedroom.

She and her husband, Scott, had started sleeping in separate rooms a few years earlier. At the time, he was driving a truck and traveled to Arkansas and Missouri on alternate days. It was more like over-the-road than local although he came home each evening. Because he was a light sleeper and had to get up at 4:30 each morning and because she had developed menopausal sleeping difficulties, she began sleeping in the second bedroom so her nightly meanderings would not disturb him.

By the time he returned to teaching last year, both of them had gotten used to sleeping alone. She was still a light, restless sleeper and got up at least once a night. And Scott was still easily disturbed.

The marriage had been deteriorating for the last couple of years anyway so separate sleeping arrangements solved other problems as well. Sarah had finally learned her attempts to express her opinions, or discuss issues that were bothering her only resulted in arguments that never ended and accomplished nothing. Most of the time now, she kept her thoughts and feelings to herself. When she didn't, there was an explosion. Otherwise, they lived peaceably although mostly going their separate ways.

Seeing her things strewn on the bed this way, solidified for her the depth of the breach between them, however. She had taken most of her things from his room months ago. She left some personal things in three small drawers of his simply because there was no more drawer space in her room and he had unused drawer space in his.

Seeing these things dumped carelessly on her bed was like hearing him verbalize the thought, "I am so far removed from caring about you I don't even want your things in my room." "How typically selfish," she thought. He had the space, she didn't.

Instinctively, she moved her wedding band from her left hand to the right. "Whatever this is," she thought, "it isn't a marriage. Never has been."

Somehow moving the ring had the effect of releasing that last foolish bit of resistance to reality that had been lodged inside her heart. Which surprised her. She thought she had experienced her "epiphany of reality" last summer when she injured her back and had to return home in the middle of their vacation.

The memory of the betrayal was still vivid in her mind.

The next planned stop on their trip had been Scott's home town and when the pain of her injury became too much they made arrangements for her to fly home so he could continue on the trip. Just outside Little Rock, they called her daughter, Caryn, to tell her she was flying from Little Rock to Nashville and that Scott would call later with her arrival time once he learned the details.

Except he forgot to call. Arriving in Nashville ensconced in a wheelchair, she waited and waited. And paged her daughter. No response. Eventually, she called Caryn's house only to discover her daughter had already gone to bed. Not hearing from Scott, she finally decided her mom had either changed her flight or made other arrangements. When Sarah called of course Caryn insisted on coming to the airport even though Sarah offered to take a cab.

Scott did call the next day to see how Sarah was but he didn't even realize what he had forgotten to do the night before until Sarah asked, "Why didn't you call Caryn with my arrival time?". "Oh, I forgot," he replied and immediately began talking about something else.

Incredulous at first, reflection finally gave way to reality. Now she thought of it as her epiphany of understanding. "I can't pretend any longer," she thought at the time. "Out of sight, out of mind."

"Like a cat," she thought.

Feeling that sharp emotional thrust in her gut when she saw the disarray in her bedroom today, however, made her realize she hadn't quite accepted the reality of the situation after all. Till now. Moving her wedding band was instinctive. And resolute.

* * * * *

From the beginning, Scott had never worn his wedding ring except sporadically, when she'd remind him. Even in the early days of their marriage. He said it was dangerous to wear anything on his fingers when he was driving a truck. "A good way to lose a finger," he said. Except he never wore it any other time either. Unless she reminded him. Eventually, she stopped reminding him and it laid on his dresser.

Then one day she thought, "Why should this lovely ring lay here on this dresser. I'll wear it." She put it on her left ring finger first, because it was a little large, and then added her own. That way, it looked like a matched set. His was a solid gold band, hers was a solid gold band with a one-half caret diamond set in the middle. "How lovely," she thought.

The diamond was from her engagement ring from her first marriage. It had been her suggestion they put it in her present wedding band. She knew Scott didn't have the money or the interest is spending money on rings and she thought it was a shame to leave it lying in a jewelry box until she died and it got passed on to one of her children. They picked a jeweler they knew and chose a low setting that would make the ring seem more like a wedding band than an engagement ring. She was delighted with the results.

Until about a year ago. The relationship was on its downward slide and she couldn't in good conscience continue to wear his ring. It mattered more somehow as the relationship deteriorated that he thought so little of her and their marriage that he wouldn't wear it himself. So she stopped wearing it for him. And put it back on his dresser top. He had never commented when she wore it and he never commented when she stopped.

She had to stop wearing it, of course. It was as though the wearing of it was evidence that she accepted the fact that the entire responsibility for the marriage relationship rested solely on her shoulders. Once this insight came to her, she could no longer wear his ring. It compromised her integrity.

She returned it to his dresser.

If he noticed, he never said.

Journal Entry, 8/13/1998

So here I am, waiting for the hair color to "set" so I can shampoo it and then be on my way.

On my way to Caryn's, where I shall spend the night and she and I will drive separately – she in her truck, me in my '85 Buick Regal – to Michigan for eight days.

Her reasons for going are strictly family-related. Grandma Sullivan is celebrating her 80 something birthday August 17th and family from everywhere are coming to honor her. Folks from South Dakota, Kim and Al from wherever they live, et cetera.

John had planned to ride up with me – though John in the car, even my car, means John driving -- regardless of what I want. But he and Drew are remodeling some rich guy's house and he's changed the plans so many times they're now charging him by the hour – $35.00 by the hour, to be exact. So he can't pass up that kind of work.

He plans to drive up next Saturday – or knowing him, he'll leave Friday after working all day -- and then get back in time for Jeremy to go to school on Monday. Sounds like a schedule for disaster to me. Hope his Guardian Angel stays on the job.

Originally, Caryn suggested she and I take a 4-5 day trip to Mackinac Island, Tahquamenon Falls, and Whitefish Pointe but things happened and now she can't. Originally, she was on an unlimited time schedule, like me, but now she has to be back by the 24th. She didn't want to spend 4 of the 8 days in Michigan with someone she sees all the time. Makes sense.

Except I was really counting on this trip. For numerous reasons. So I asked Lisa is she could get a babysitter and she and I would go. Considering I haven't been alone with my daughter since she was 13 years old – for any length of time, quality time – it seemed like a good idea to me.

Getting babysitters for the children is, of course, presenting nearly insurmountable problems. Seems like her dad could keep her children for a few days. Hahahahaha. Big joke.

He made a beautiful wooden cradle for Caryn and brought it to her recently. When she was still pregnant the second time. Before she miscarried. Again. I cried when I saw it. First because I knew it was a labor of love and I was touched by this evidence of his love for his daughter, his child. Then I cried for a very different reason. And wished it was standing before me so I could say, "but where's Lisa's cradle?"

Keeping the children for 4-5 days so she and I could make this trip could be her cradle.

Except that will never happen.

Apparently Josie is now asking the same question Caryn raised. Why would Dawn come up here to see all of us and then take off for four days?

But my agenda is not her agenda.

My reasons for going to Michigan initially were two-fold; one to visit my children and their children, and two, to research the material I need for these essays I writing. Which means trips to Cass City/Kingston where my dad's people are from. Plus going to the downtown Detroit library where an entire floor, I believe, is maintained by the Detroit Historical Society. Everything I ever needed to know about Detroit is probably garnered here.

Then, too, I want to get pictures of mine and my dad's old neighborhood. Where Tom says I can no longer go. If I wish to live.

But I still plan to do it. Scott suggested I contact a cab company, explain my dilemma, and get a black driver either to go and take the pictures I want, or maybe I could ride along and do it myself. We'll see.

So right now I'm waiting on my hair.

And feeling very sorry for myself. Or just depressed about things in general, I guess.

I thought life was supposed to get easier, not harder, as you grew older.

This past year has been difficult for lots of reasons. Which is why I was so looking forward to the Mackinac/Tahquamenon/Whitefish Pointe trip. It was going to be my reward for surviving all this mess.

Whatever remaining tendrils of hope or wishful thinking I had about Scott's and my relationship were obliterated once and for all when he "forgot" to tell Caryn what flight I would be arriving on last year when I got my back injury, the herniated disk. Subsequent similar frequent examples have further proved it.

He wants out. Yesterday his words were, "as soon as possible." He was ranting and raving. I didn't interrupt or ask what he meant. When he finished, I just said, "You are the most ungrateful person I have ever met."

It is very frightening to be 60 years old, unsure of what kind of income I can produce job-wise, and know that I'm it. For taking care of me. Nobody but me is going to do it.

Of course, one big reason I wanted to remarry – in addition to being in love – was for the financial security I hoped it would provide me in my advancing years. Hahahahaha again.

Life has repeatedly taught me that, no matter what, the bottom line is, it is and will always be a man's world. And when they get through doing whatever it is they want to do with you, you'd better be prepared to float your own boat. 'Cause when the chips are down, they're not going to do it for you.

Smart is the generation of women who came after me who acted responsibly with this knowledge and got education and careers that enabled them to create their own financial security. Hard though it was and is on them to wear so many different hats.

SARAH'S STORY

Some of my generation of women figured this out. But most of us didn't.

* * * * *

I'm not depressed just because of my own situation. Though at times it really gets to me. But everywhere I turn in this family, I see problems. John, and Lisa, and Caryn and Randy. Randy is a big POD too sometimes And Randy is one of the good guys. But he is so CONTROLLING. I can't believe some of the things Caryn has told me. Actually, we are ALL Controllers/Take Charge People.

Everywhere I turn, all I see is mess. Emotional mess.

* * * * *

Here I am getting ready to go on this trip. Several times during the past six weeks I have asked Scott to please check out my car and let me know if anything needs fixing. (I recently paid him back EVERYTHING he spent on this car. Even though it took getting money out of my meager retirement fund.)

He said everything was okay.

Recently the oil light has been going on – occasionally. Only when the car has been running awhile and only when I come to a stop light. If I put the car in neutral and give it some gas, the light goes off.

At first Scott said he would never drive a car if the oil light was coming on. At the time I had planned to go to Jackson and he didn't think it was wise. But I went anyway.

Then he changed the oil in it and it stopped doing it.

Two days ago, the light came on again as I was returning home from the Y.

He and I, and me and Tom, and me and John, and Tom and Scott have talked about it. When I get to Michigan Tom is going to put the car up on his rack and look it over. Scott's first response was that it might need an oil pump. Tom says this is very unlikely. Worst case scenario is it's something in the motor and you would have to take the motor out of the car and literally take it apart to find out the problem.

If that's what he thinks it is, it would be easier just to buy another motor and put it in. But we're talking $1300 if Tom did it. And that wouldn't count any money for him. Plus it's an all-day job. I wouldn't expect him to be able to do this while I'm up there. But if somehow he could, I still would have to come up with another $200 at least because it would take him all day.

So that's one problem.

Scott said the left front tire. Looked kind of worn and suggested I take it to the corner tire shop and get another $15 tire. So I did. They noticed the tire they put on a few weeks ago was already beginning to wear and suggested I get a front-end alignment.

A front-end alignment was part of the estimate for the damage to my car(*). But when I finally got the check from the insurance company, Scott said it was foolish to spend a thousand dollars fixing the car with either of the repair shops that gave us the estimates because we could get it done cheaper.

So I'm holding on to the money until –

In the meantime, I told Scott I planned to take the car to Dunlap & Kyle this morning for the alignment. I called them and they said it would cost $39.95 or $49.95, depending on my car.

He went out and looked under the hood and came back and said, well, the "somethings" are dry rotted. They may try and say you need to replace them for their alignment to take. Replacing them would cost you about $300-$400. So don't let them do that.

I can't believe this.

So later I ask him about this. I ask why, since I've been asking him for several weeks what, if anything, needed to be done to my car, does he tell me two days before I leave about this problem.

He got angry. Surprise, surprise. Started talking about well, if we had tons of money I could just take your car to so and so and such and such and get this done and that done and on and on. But ever since you left Steiner-Liff, and started working for yourself, you said you were going to pay $200 a month on Wachovia. So you did for a while. But you stopped paying any utilities and groceries so what it amounts to is I'm paying for everything myself. And I can't afford to pay to fix the car the way it needs to be fixed.

You sit around here and write this great novel that no one wants to read and you play with your genealogy stuff, which doesn't accomplish anything as far as money goes –

He just went on and on.

Whenever he goes into these tirades, he talks as though I just sit around twiddling my thumbs watching TV and laying around the house.

He does NOTHING around this house. I do all the yard work-- which I happen to like. But it would be nice if he helped once in a while, especially when limbs need picking up, and other stuff that needs doing besides just mowing. Bush trimming, carting stuff to the dump, etc.

The wooden carpet strips are still showing in half the places around the room where we took up the carpet a year ago, for God's sake. I got what I could but there are places where I can't move the furniture to get at it.

The cupboard I had built – and paid for – in the kitchen has never been painted. It won't get painted, of course, unless do it.

He can't even scrub a tub or sink – pink scum builds in the tub until I finally can't stand it and clean it. I only take stand up showers so I ignore as long as I can.

He can't even find food in the refrigerator. Home-cooked food that is prepared weekly so that all he has to do is open the container and put it on his plate and heat it in the microwave. Recently I moved some cheese and lunch meat to make room for several containers of food I cooked. That evening he asked me what happened to his cheese and lunch meat. It was no longer in the place it had been. I went into the kitchen, opened the frig, and looked. It was on a different shelf but easy to see standing in front of the open frig.

Please God, let me find a good job.

Let me publish articles/essays/books, whatever. Let me pay him back every cent he claims I owe.

Help me figure out how to support myself. So I can tell HIM to hit the road.

If I didn't have my name on the deed to this house, I have no doubt he would have tried to get me out of here.

I think he tries now. By all this ugly talk.

But I'm not leaving.

At least not yet.

*****

He knows why I left Steiner-Liff. It was the pits. He agreed when I told him that's what I wanted to do.

He agreed with me when I bought this computer stuff and tried to get my own business going. I was doing okay. Very labor intensive typing depositions, etc. My hands were getting in really bad shape. Not carpel tunnel. Arthritis. The joints in my fingers were bulging. They've improved now but some are still "bumpy" like old ladies' fingers. Maybe because I'm an old lady now.

He liked the genealogy work I did on his family.

He seemed to approve of my stories. Bragged about my writing sometimes.

Of course, since last July, when I got injured, he's been more critical. Done NOTHING to help me during the course of that injury. Anne, Caryn, and Jay helped me more than he did.

You might say he practically didn't lift a finger.

Oh, wait. He and Bo DID cook dinner one night.

So finally I get well enough to try and get back to work. I end up at CH working part-time hoping I can continue to write or type here at home in addition to working somewhere else.

The job at CH takes more and more of my time. I LOVE the work and think if I do a really super job, et cetera et cetera, I'll get a raise to a decent wage.

Doesn't happen. So I take a gamble. Advise them I have to have more money or leave.

They let me leave.

All the while I worked there, Scott complained about how little money I earned.

So now I have left there. Hopefully, to make more money.

But I planned a trip for a few days before I get back out there in the rat race.

And the crabbing continues.

I applied for a job with the Tennessee Board of Regents. I thought they would have called me for an interview this week before I had to leave for Michigan. They haven't called. Don't know if it's because they didn't like what they saw on my resume or if it's just the slow wheels of government.

Maybe I'll get a chance to interview when I return.

Otherwise, I plan to sign up with AccountTemps. And take odds and ends of accounting clerk jobs. Till I learn enough to be able to handle "office manager" of a small office. Or something.

* * * * *

Gotta wash this stuff off and get to Caryn's before the traffic hits.

(*) A few weeks ago I was going through an intersection on a North directed street on the green light when a car in the West directed street made his right turn, against the light, and hit my car in the left front tire area. Fortunately, we were both going 5-10 MPH.

December 15, 1998

Dear Friends,

It's that time of year again, so here goes.

At the end of July I quit my part-time job at the drug and alcohol rehabilitation center. I loved the work but not the pay. I offered to resign or stay – and work longer hours – for more money. They opted for the first choice. I went to Michigan for a couple of weeks and then signed on with AccountTemps here in Nashville.

I recently started a long-term assignment with a cement company (they have 9 plants here in Tennessee and Corporate offices in Louisville and somewhere in Indiana). They are in a computer conversion drowning in a sea of confusion and misplaced papers. Voila. Super-organizer Sarah to the rescue. (I am one of three temps and we can't decide which of us is the most anal retentive re our compulsion for orderliness/neatness). It looks as though they may eventually offer me a permanent position but I'm not sure doing what. If it's computer accounting, I would be interested, otherwise not. Today they sent everyone home with a 13-lb ham and a 13-lb turkey. It was thoughtful of them to include me. I think it's a good company.

When I recovered from my herniated disk last year, I found I could no longer sit at my computer and type for 8-10 hours a day preparing depositions. My hands, not my back, hurt too much; arthritis, I guess. New technology eliminates 75-85% of the typing and I'm trying to get proficient in the programs to allow me to continue this work. I would like to be able to do it evenings and weekends and still keep a day job for the security and benefits.

I know one thing. Until I had that herniated disc, I never knew you could feel such physical pain and live. Once I realized the pain wasn't going to kill me, I stopped being afraid. But it was a long recovery. And I don't ever want to do that again!

Since then I've come to believe that becoming self-supporting is a necessity, not an option. At 60 plus, such a realization is kind of scary but when Scott put me on that plane in a wheelchair in July of 1997 and then "forgot" to call my daughter and tell her what time my flight was arriving in Nashville it simply confirmed what I already knew.

We just never know where life will lead us, do we? Such a blessing. Mostly when I talk to God these days I just ask Him to give me the strength and wisdom to do whatever it is that I have to do. The fact that I still have my parents, relatively healthy and productive children, and reasonable health myself seems to me a lot to be grateful for. Like most people my age, I've had a measure of hard times but I know too that those hard times have made me a stronger person. My folks are 86 now and I know one of these days I'm going to have to draw upon that strength to get through losing them. And whatever else comes along.

John and Kim separated a couple of years ago; then they got back together. My gut told me it was only a matter of time, however, before she left again. And she did. So they're divorced now. John has joint custody of their son, Jeremy. He is a wonderful father. Kim got married about a week after the divorce, I think. John always was and continues to be my ray of son-shine. Both my boys seem to have all of Jerry's good qualities. This trauma has made John a better man and person, however. He has more compassion and tolerance than before. Even for his liberal old mom.

All my kids tease me unmercifully and call me their wacky liberal mom. John was listening to one of my lengthy messages to him one day and jotted a note to himself – which I later saw – that said "mom is goofy". I love it! I keep telling them I'm working very hard at becoming totally eccentric in my old age. Recently John programmed his answering machine to say "Hello. Now you say something." The first time I called after that of course I said "Something, here" which evolved to "Mrs. Goofy Something."

John is the sound engineer for Billy Dean, a country-pop, pop-country singer; I'm not sure which. Not hard-core country, in other words. A few months ago he met a singer from Cincinnati. She's here visiting him through Tuesday of this week working on a demo. I think he's falling in love. But another sound engineer (a woman) had previously asked if she could come and stay with him for a few days while she looks for work and an apartment. She arrives on Wednesday! She quit her job in Florida and expects to makes some connections here in Nashville. He said she seems to be quite mad about him. He doesn't quite know what to do with either one of them at this point. I hope he will be cautious. So does he. He confides in me the way daughters do. I love it! Plus, he is one of the "goodest" people I know.

Caryn and Randy bought their second home – in Portland, Tennessee – earlier this year. Thirty-five miles from Nashville. Their first house was five miles from me. This one is an old house with lots of room and lots of fireplaces – and lots of work to be done. It sits on 3-1/2 acres on the prettiest street in town. They also have a peach orchard. With two hundred trees! Caryn works in the securities division of First American Bank, Bowling Green office. Randy works at Opryland, repairs old houses, plays guitar and composes and sings contemporary Christian music, hoping for the Big Break.

Lisa and her two children, Leila and Andrew, (sans Mo and/or Steve,) now live in Richmond, Michigan. It's a pretty little town too. She works for a chiropractor now and an insurance company on Thursdays (her day off from the chiropractor). Plus she has a horse! A retired thoroughbred race horse, a young filly. The reason she's retired is because she wasn't winning races. So they sold her. Lisa gives riding lessons on weekends in exchange for boarding the horse. The farm she boards the horse at is affiliated with the March of Dimes. In addition to other classes and events, they offer riding lessons to handicapped children.

I'm planning to go to Michigan for the month of March and stay with her children so she can go to Fort Wayne and take a March of

Dimes sanctioned crash course in teaching handicapped children to ride. Between now and then she has to study the books. The month in Fort Wayne will be testing and demonstrating what she's learned. It's going to be hard to find time to study but of all my strong, determined kids, Lisa has always been the most. Strong-willed and determined, that is. I hope she can put those traits to use now. If she can, this is a wonderful opportunity for her to become financially stable.

Tom, Josie, and their three children still live in Royal Oak. I can't believe how congested everything is around there. I think they would like to move further out but don't know if or when that might happen. Josie talks about it more than Tom. Tom feels the responsibility of owning his own mechanic business. He seems to be doing okay but of course it's all on his shoulders; the only benefits coming from his labor. Just last year he hooked up with a guy who has an immense steel and concrete building near Rochester/Sixteen Mile (I think). He restores vintage cars. Tom leases space from him and the guy frequently sends business Tom's way so that's another plus.

That trip to Michigan last August? I was there about 12 days and Caryn and John were there part of that time. I babysat all SIX grandkids one Saturday night so my four could go out together! (You should have seen the instructions they gave me! Imagine. An old pro like me. As if you ever forget. I put them all to bed at 7 p.m.! . . . Just kidding.)

Anyway, I spent a few days with Lisa up in Richmond and then went on up to Cass City and Kingston, Michigan. Which is where my dad is from. And I had never been. I poked around and talked with people, relatives, etc. and got some more information and pictures for the stories I'm writing. In Kingston, I got pictures of the brick house and hardware store my great-grandfather built. The cornerstone of the hardware store still says, "The Hopps Block 1901". Kingston was having a "festival" the following weekend I was there and the city fathers had produced a booklet commemorating the event. Additionally, the antique store had a book on the history of the town from 1857-1982. I bought both and got some great information and pictures about my great-grandfather. I had so much fun! I wish I could afford to spend all my time poking around little towns and talking to old characters and writing about it all.

Maybe some day.

So that wraps up another year. May health and happiness be yours in '99.

There is Life After Herniation. And It Is GOOD!

Love,
Sarah

Journal Entry, 04/03/1999

I am getting ready to go to Jackson to visit my folks.

Just woke from my nightmare-like dream. So vivid. Called Caryn to tell her. She agreed I should write it down. Maybe some day I will understand it.

This is what I remember.

I don't know what went before. This is where I became "aware" of the story. My current real life next door neighbor's yard was next door in the dream. Brandy (*) had been missing. Where I remember the dream beginning (although I had the sense of it being in progress prior to this) is me looking out the window and seeing the neighbor's yard with a hole in the back yard. At first it wasn't that big but during the dream it kept getting bigger.

At first it was about two feet wide. Somehow I knew it was deep – 10-15 feet.

I look out the window. It is almost evening but still light. I see Brandy. He is in the hole but nearly to the top. He is covered in dirt and mud and struggling to reach the top of the hole. And get out. Somehow I know he has done this many times. And is doing it once again. He struggles and almost makes it. But finally falls back.

I am relieved to know where he's been. And concerned. But it seems natural to think we'll go over there tomorrow morning and get a ladder or something and help get him out.

Now it is the next day. Tom and John are about 10-12 years old. They seem to be running around the neighborhood trying to find a ladder.

My first thought when I realize Brandy is trapped down in this hole is that we could put a rope down and if we could somehow get him to grab it with his teeth, we could pull and he could claw (like he had been doing for how long?) his way to the top. But I figured we wouldn't be able to make him understand to grab the rope with his teeth. So that's when I decided we needed a ladder.

Why we can't find a ladder, I don't know. As part of the dream it seems I am aware that we make many unsuccessful attempts to find a ladder.

The hole is getting bigger. Now it is about the size of three cars wide and I can easily see down in it. The bottom is narrower than the top. Meaning the sides are slanted.

Now Jerry is down there. I don't know his age but his hair is not grey. He is stocky, though.

Suddenly he leans back against a side of the hole. As though he is in pain or having some kind of physical problem. As part of the dream, I wonder if he's having a heart attack.

I am the observer in all this. Although I sense that I have been directing efforts to get Brandy out.

Now there are filing cabinets along some of the sides of the hole. And Tom and John are down there now too. They and their dad seem to think pulling some of the drawers open helter-skelter would make like stair-steps and Brandy (and them?) could climb out that way.

I "think" this is not a good idea. I am concerned that the open drawers will make the filing cabinets topple over.

I don't know if I convey this to them or just think it in my observer mode.

Sure enough, one of the cabinets falls over. It lands on Lisa. Suddenly, she is down there too. Where she has been till now, I don't know but now she is there. She is about 4-5 years old.

Jerry doesn't seem to realize the cabinet has fallen on top of her. I try to tell him. He almost doesn't believe me. But moves it enough to realize she is under there.

I can see her face. She is in pain and frightened. Her lower lip is trembling and her arms and/or legs are shaking also.

I am trying to make Jerry understand that she is hurt but he doesn't seem to realize it. He seems to be carelessly pulling her from under the cabinet. Her constant eye contact with me makes me know she is hurt and frightened.

All I want to do is grab her up in my arms and hold her and comfort her.

Where Caryn has been in all this I don't know.

That's when I wake up.

(*) dog we had when we lived in Huntington Woods, Michigan

During the summer of 1999, Scott moved out. Back to Missouri. He wanted to go. I wanted to stay. So we agreed that I would buy the house from him.

As always when faced with life-changing events, it helps me sort through my emotions and come to terms with outcomes by writing about them.

The result: two more essays for my memoir.

October 1999

– CASTING PEARLS –

"Who owns the Harley?" I asked as I entered the apartment full of Parents Without Partners congregating for their monthly Sunday Pot Luck. "That's gotta be Scott," said Susan as she pointed to a slender guy standing across the room. I headed straight for him.

I guess you could say our mutual interest in motorcycles spawned a friendship that quickly became much more. For my part, I instantly saw the motorcycle as evidence of a free spirit.

As someone who had been a responsible, sensible, proper married lady for 22 years, helping raise four children, almost daily preparing meals for six, carpooler extraordinaire, PTSAer, scout leader, yada, yada, yada, I was more than ready to try some of that 'free spirit' pose myself.

Finding out this guy also had a '67 Buick Gransport that he raced yearly at Bowling Green as a member of the Gransport Club of America was just another piece that fit the image I was quickly forming of this man as someone I wanted to get to know. And emulate.

So began our 14-year odyssey. Now ended.

We did have some times, though. Especially in the first six years or so. Many of them riding that bike; a 1450 Harley Sportster. Green with yellow pin striping and black leather bags. No faring to spoil "the look".

In those early months and years, when we both were playing the game according to the unspoken rules, we had some fun alright. Coming home from work we'd jump into jeans and helmets (sweaters, jackets in the fall) and just take off. Two free spirits. Riding in the wind. Going maybe a hundred miles in and around the country surrounding Nashville before we got back home again. Stopping at a roadside restaurant for a meal or snack.

SARAH'S STORY

Arriving home hours later, tired and happy. But not too tired for sex. Hoo-ha! And then off to sleep. Me curled up spoon-fashion behind him.

I remember riding behind him, thinking, "I can't believe I'm doing this. Me. Sarah. Middle-aged me. I love it, love it, love it!."

We joined the Harley Davidson Hog Club of Nashville and claimed to be Nashville's oldest teenagers.

One summer Saturday the club met at 6 a.m. and we caravanned – 45 bikes long – to the Rifle River to spend most of the day canoeing. Scott and I got separated from our group late that afternoon and I found out later he felt the same isolation and momentary fear I did as we lost track of our companions and paddled down this unfamiliar river that looked suddenly menacing with the sun dropping lower and lower in the sky overhead. A few minutes later, however, we rounded a bend in the river and, just as it was supposed to be, there was the dock a short distance ahead where we were to return our canoes. The world that had tipped suddenly askew fell back into place once more.

Another time, in the fall when the leaves were at their peak color, the club rode to Cherokee, North Carolina. Three hundred miles. Round trip. On a weekend. Precisely, 4:30 a.m. Saturday morning till 9 p.m. Sunday night.

My seat for this trip was about 18 inches long and 8 inches wide! Numb bumb. I know I invented new ways to ride shotgun on that trip. (Go down on your knees on the floor. Sit back on your haunches. Now imagine that position atop the rear seat on a motorcycle). Eventually you try it one leg at a time.

Another option was to let my legs just hang – not using the rear foot pedals. Short is good sometimes; a taller person wouldn't have that option. Letting my legs hang that way redistributed the weight on my bottom slightly. Sometimes I placed my hands behind me on the metal strips of the back rest and leaned back. That also changed my weight distribution slightly. Anything for variety.

Returning to Nashville that Sunday evening--the temperature had dropped suddenly about the time we got to Chattanooga – it started sleeting about 45 minutes from Nashville. Not fun. Some of us stopped at a tavern that served hamburgers and beer before going home.

There were people of all ages in the club. Our interest in riding negated age differences and vocational interests. People of varying socio-economic rank came together for one reason. They loved Harleys. And they loved to ride.

One couple we made friends with during the trip was about 20 years younger than us. I don't remember what the guy looked like but the girl was about 25, cute, with long blond hair which she kept pinned up under her helmet. When we stopped for breaks, she let it hang loose down her back.

Scott was quite taken with this couple. Even then I realized it was really the girl who fascinated him.

On more than one occasion afterwards, if we got to talking about motorcycles and the trips we took et cetera, he talked about this girl and the effect she had on him. She rode in back, like all the women on the trip. He would speak of her "free" personality. Evidenced to him on the trip in the manner she sat, the movements she made, the attitude she had; all of which bespoke to him of this young, free-spirited woman.

Scott always spoke openly and freely with me in our early years about the different relationships he'd had with women. And I told him of my own experiences, although there wasn't much to tell compared to his stories. I liked hearing about his relationships and experiences. It fit the picture I had of him as this free spirit. In a way, I was envious. I think part of my falling in love with him was my imagining that somehow by just being near him some of it would rub off on me.

I tried to make that happen. But that's another story. And it didn't work anyway.

But getting back to my point. About the girl. Scott was obviously taken with her. I knew from stories he had told me about his past experiences that he was always attracted to women who exhibited freedom in their behavior and attitudes. Probably most men are but maybe most of them don't talk about it to their partners or admit these feelings. Scott thought, and I agreed, it stemmed from his restrictive, guilt-ridden childhood as a PK (preacher's kid).

I didn't see any of this as a threat to me or our relationship. I found it stimulating to have him share this information with me. So hearing him talk this way about the girl did not bother me. It didn't make me jealous. Even then, however, I knew something was out of kilter. I didn't understand and realize exactly what it was or the significance of it then. Twelve years later I do.

Pretend to be an observer on this motorcycle trip. You see all of us riding – guy in front, girl behind.

You see the young blond sitting behind her man. You see me sitting behind Scott. **We both are acting the same way.** Comfortable and secure, rearranging our bodies on the bike to compensate for the small seating area available to us. Free spirits in the wind. There is a difference, of course. One is 25 years old, the other 45. One is with Scott, one is not.

Scott had the very thing he was enamored of but didn't have the sense to know it. Or the awareness. In other words, clueless. I didn't know it at the time, but his response to that girl was a first but excellent example of why our relationship ultimately failed.

To have a precious jewel and treat it like riverbed stone is, after all, unforgivable.

I can think of one thing worse.

To not know.

November 1999

– An Ending ... of Sorts –

It has been quite a day.

I'd been nervous driving to the lawyer's office this morning. Anticipation coupled with a niggling sense of anxiety that, even at this late moment when everything was supposedly in order, some thing, unplanned or unaccounted for, would prevent my mortgage closing. Buying a house on my own at sixty-one was a sobering undertaking; after three months of paper processing, it was hard for me to believe it was actually happening.

The process had been unnecessarily complicated because Scott's lawyer had insisted he be free and clear of the house before she would allow him to sign the divorce papers. She allow him??? It was His business and My business.

I wouldn't have involved lawyers in the first place but once he hired one, I had no choice. As it was, my lawyer recapitulated by saying *I* could not sign the divorce papers until the house was in **MY** name.

We didn't need any lawyers. Couldn't AFFORD any lawyers. We both understood the marriage was over; he wanted to leave, I wanted to stay. No conflict. Just a matter of me buying him out.

And therein lay the glitch. He bought the house before our marriage so the mortgage was in his name only. We had to get him free and clear of his loan and then I had to get my own. The easy thing, the simple thing, would have been to get the divorce, have him quit claim the deed over to me, and then I would get a mortgage in my name only.

Thanks to legal expertise, however, he now had to be present for my closing; first to sign the mortgage and then to sign a waiver relinquishing any claim on the property in question. All because we are still technically married. After signing, he will take a copy of the appropriate papers back to his lawyer, who will then allow him to sign the divorce papers, who will then send them to my lawyer, who will then send them to me for my signature. Ya-da ya-da ya-da.

Thanks to his lawyer's "conditions", his name ended up being on **MY** mortgage. Albeit momentarily. Which was exactly what neither of us wanted. And he had to drive all the way from Missouri to do it!

But I didn't know any of this before the closing.

* * * * *

I check my watch as I pull into the parking lot of the lawyer's office. The closing is set for 11:30 a.m. and I am a few minutes early. The lawyer's assistant ushers me in to an office where Scott is already waiting.

"I didn't think you were here yet," I remarked as I sat down. "I didn't see your car."

"I drove a friend's van; it will hold more of my stuff than my El Camino," Scott replied.

"That makes sense," I said. "Where's your friend?"

"She's waiting in the van."

"Ah," I replied, comprehending at last.

Moments later, the lawyer arrives. I sign a myriad of papers; Scott signs a few. It takes about 45 minutes. As the lawyer explains what we are doing, I realize why Scott is here and what he is signing.

I mention this as we leave but I don't think he gets it. I resent the fact his name is, after all, on my mortgage, but trust the waiver does, in fact, absolve him from any obligation as well as any claim to my property. I head for the tire store to get two new front tires and a front-end alignment and Scott takes his copies of the papers to his lawyer's office. He has offered to stop back at the tire store to pick me up since it will take an hour or so for them to fix my car.

We drive back to the house. I knew he had planned to stop by to get more of his stuff. I just didn't know a woman would be with him. But it's her van, after all. I didn't even know he had a woman friend. But that doesn't surprise me, either.

He introduces us as I get in the back seat. It could be awkward but isn't. We're grown-ups, after all. She didn't meet him till he moved to Missouri, after all.

Scott pulls up to the side of the house to make it easier to load the van. I go around to the front door and once inside come around to unlock the side door. They come in, Scott exclaims over how big the cat has gotten, and heads for the basement.

Sally is small in stature. A little pudgy like me but in different places. Tight jeans and turtleneck reveal little bulges here and there. Salt and pepper hair and dark eyes. Attractive.

Scott comes back upstairs. As I direct them to the piles and boxes I have accumulated for him, we talk. Ironically, I realize this is a woman I could like; someone I could be friends with. Under different circumstances. She is friendly and speaks intelligently.

I learn she is self-employed; sells real estate and is a tax accountant. She goes on to say she is a Pentecostal Christian and has been a minister for 20 years. But recently left the ministry. Because she can't be a minister and drink and dance and she has recently discovered both. I am dumbfounded! Scott the Atheist coupled with a Fundamentalist! Unbelievable.

She also is newly divorced – six months ago. As she speaks of the details of the marriage and divorce I hear remnants of pain in her voice although she says it is behind her now. That sisterhood of woman bonding thing rises up in me and I blurt out, "but you're so needy right now. You need time to heal."

"Actually it's been two years since we split up. It's just that the divorce became final six months ago."

She talks about a husband who was undemonstrative, who didn't show her any affection. The more she talks, the more I feel drawn to her and the more I feel the need to warn her. Warn her of what? It's none of my business. Recognizing this does not subdue the feeling.

She says she and Scott met about six months ago and haven't stopped talking since. How familiar this sounds.

I tell her, "Well, Scott will tell you he wants an independent woman. Beware! He only wants you to be independent as long as you agree with his point of view." Scott is standing nearby and I say it in a joking manner – I hope. They both grin so I guess it's okay that I said it.

I continue by saying, "Which I have decided must just be a male thing."

"I think you're right," she replies and smiles also. "We've had some of those kinds of conversations already."

"Well, don't back down," I say.

"Oh, I won't; I'm good at defending myself. He knows that already."

Sounds more and more like this is a potentially serious relationship. I feel concern for what I perceive to be this woman's needs because I have no doubt they will remain unfulfilled. What is this pain I'm beginning to feel? Why do I feel so protective of her? She says she has dated quite a few men during the past two years. I sense that she is looking for someone to love. And to be loved. I know the feeling. I was there. Fourteen years ago. It didn't happen.

We are alone for a few minutes when Scott goes back to the basement.

As we stand emptying clothes from what once was his closet, I decide to speak what's in my heart. "Please don't misunderstand but I feel the need to talk to you woman-to-woman. I don't wish Scott any harm. I just feel the need to warn you. If you just want a friend, a sexual buddy, then you probably won't be disappointed. But if you're looking for something more, please be careful. Scott himself told me in the early months of our relationship that a woman he once dated for nine months told him, 'Scott, you're a taker.' I learned she was right."

"Whatever it is that did or didn't happen to Scott as a child has made him the way he is. It's why we all are the way we are, of course, but with Scott, what this amounts to is, I don't think he knows how to love. It's not that he's intentionally selfish or unkind. But he is the most self-absorbed person I have ever known. And hasn't a clue as to how to be a father or a husband. Clueless is what he is."

Then I tell her about his daughter's wedding and how he failed to show up at almost the last minute. He was driving over the road at the time and called me to say he would have to cut his run short and it might jeopardize his job and he thought he would probably just be in the way anyway and what did I think he should do? (His ex-wife and daughter had rented a hotel room for us, bought flowers for me and him, rented him a tux. They were expecting him to walk her down the aisle, for god's sake!)

I told her by this point in the marriage I was tired of being the manager, the mother, of making his decisions for him, so I told him he had to do what he thought best. What he thought best was not to go. It broke his daughter's heart and she called in tears two days before the wedding. Scott was still out on the road and I had to talk to her. I felt horrible. And wished for her sake I had talked him into doing the right thing – at least one more time.

Just then I heard Scott's footsteps on the stairs and tried once again to assure Sally I wasn't trying to be vindictive. "I just have the feeling you may be looking for something that isn't going to be there."

"No, no, I've wondered about some of this myself. I'm glad to know."

* * * * *

By the time the tire shop called to say my car was ready, Sally and Scott were just about finished loading up the things they planned to take. Scott has to return in November for the court date for the divorce and will get the rest of his things then.

We all piled into the van one more time and they dropped me off at the tire store.

As I prepared to exit the van, Sally said, "I was a little nervous about meeting you but hoped it would be okay. And it was."

"Me, too," I said. "But there's no reason for me to have bad feelings toward you. What happened between Scott and me happened before he ever knew you. You had nothing to do with it."

"Well, that's how I hoped you'd feel. My best friend had an affair with my husband so that's the last thing I would ever do to another woman," Sally replied.

"Have a safe trip; I wish you well," I said as I exited the van and headed to the tire store. I wrote my check, left the store, and drove home with a little knot of pain and sadness rumbling around deep inside my guts. I didn't exactly know why.

Then I figured it out.

Scott is looking for a connection. Of sorts. He was looking for it when he ran into me. Who was looking and hoping and praying. To be needed. To be loved.

He found the real thing but he didn't know it and he didn't take care of it. And then he lost it.

Me, I'm not looking anymore.

Scott still is.

He's run into someone who's looking and hoping and praying . . .

I have to stop now. There is a pain behind my eyes and it is spreading to my throat and moving down to squeeze around my heart.

But Life Goes On . . .

Let the poetry flow . . .

SON OF MY HEART
(For Tom)

First-born son of my heart
son of my life
never was a child awaited
with more anticipation and
received with such love

Do you remember how I sang
Tombo, Tombo
Where You Gonna Go-We-O
and all those other
silly childhood songs

I yearn to hold that little baby
just once more
to touch him with my love

Pliable, happy, easily directed
you were such a good baby,
I knew I wanted to have a dozen
more like you

Years later I realized
it was less my expertise and more
your inherent nature that made you
Such a delightful, good-natured baby

I'll never forget the time you were bitten
by a child during social hour after church
I think it hurt me and grandpa much more
than it hurt you

I yearn to hold that little baby
just once more
to touch him with my love

As your brother and sisters came along
your dad and I expected too much
we took advantage of your innate sense
of responsibility and goodness

We expected you to be our little man
setting standards much too demanding
always though, you tried to comply

I yearn to hold that little boy
just once more
to touch him with my love

Moving to Tennessee
taking you from your friends
at First Baptist Church
uprooted you all much more
than we realized at the time
Yet I know we hoped it would be
a new beginning for us all.

First-born son of my heart
son of my life
I yearn for another chance

A chance to be more patient
more understanding
more appreciative
of the kind, gentle little boy who
too quickly grew into a man
A man of integrity and honor

fulfilling the promise and potential
of the delightful child of long ago

I yearn to hug that man
once more
to touch him with my love

For now, I write these simple words
and hope my feelings
which are constant and forever
will rise up off the page
and touch him with my love.

A RAY OF SONSHINE
(For John)

Little John
do you remember when we called you that
to distinguish you from your grandpa
for whom you were named

Too soon you became Big John
then Bigger John
when in your teens you towered
far above your namesake

A ray of sonshine in my life . . .
I remember when you were ten or so
racing home from school
running to the frig to gulp down
a large glass of orange juice

I'm just the luckiest kid, you said
Why, I asked
Because I could hardly wait to get home
to see if there was some orange juice left
and when I got here – there it was!

A ray of sonshine in my life . . .

That's how I thought of you
full of the joy of life
sure that something wonderful
was just around the corner
of your childhood world

One of the dearest treasures of my life
is the note you wrote when you were seven
and had been sent to bed early
punishment for some childhood misdeed

I picked up the paper lying outside
your closed bedroom door
and read these words –

I found out that you love Caryn
more than me and Tom
Becus we have to go to bed right away
and Caryn gets to stay up

When I turned the note over
I found a dreadful indictment,
which said

I Don't Like You

Never was I hurt or offended
by your righteous indignation
Always have I cherished this
now ragged little piece of paper
as a precious memory of your childhood
concrete evidence that you were

A ray of sonshine in my life . . .

Now you are grown
A man with a wife and child of your own
Because of who and what you are

living your life with integrity
practicing justice and honor in your work
demonstrating thoughtfulness and love
in your personal relationships
you are still . . .

A ray of sonshine in my life.

I AM BLESSED
For Caryn

I am blessed

My tears this day flow
from mixed emotions
and my heart is overflowing
as I gaze at the beautiful bride
who is my daughter

Love, happiness and pride
fill my heart for this child
love of my life, heart of my heart
as she stands at the altar
gazing thoughtfully and lovingly
at the man standing by her side
I am blessed

Always prudent and thoughtful
when considering decisions and choices
of life-changing magnitude
she stands before us now
in anticipation of the journey
which lies ahead

My heart is filled with thankfulness
as I think of the happiness and joy
she has brought to my life
a contented happy baby
a thoughtful loving child

a young woman who shares with me
the closeness and communication
often reserved for best friends
I am blessed.

TENDER SHOULDERS
For Lisa

I stare at my daughter's shoulders
revealed as they are by the dress
it's deep cranberry color emphasizing
the porcelain quality of her skin
and dramatizing the long auburn hair

Tender shoulders of a
vulnerable woman-child
Matron-of-honor she stands
somber and thoughtful
waiting to present the wedding ring
at the designated time in the service
of her sister's wedding

Tender shoulders of a
vulnerable woman-child
Conceal the independence and determination
pushing her since childhood to prove
"I can take care of myself"
rushing headlong into life and love
oblivious of the consequences

Tender shoulders of a
vulnerable woman-child
Your beautiful vulnerable shoulders
do not seem strong enough to carry
the weight of responsibility you bear

And my mother's heart longs
to reach out and crush you to my breast
to hold you in my arms
as I did in the long-ago time
of your childhood
when I had the privilege and
the power to keep you safe.

Which gave birth to . . .

— Tales from "The Woods" ---
1994

"Here they come. Run!"

Suddenly six teenagers broke ranks and scattered in five different directions. It was nine p.m. on a summer evening in Huntington Woods. The year was 1979.

Tom ran through the Hall's yard and hid in one of their bushes. Pat ran two houses further down the street and hid behind three large garbage cans sitting by the side door of Schaeffer's house. John headed across the street, jumped a shrub fence, and hid behind the large fireplace chimney located on one side of McGowan's house. Rob sprinted back the way they had come one house finding cover behind a stack of fireplace logs neatly arranged by the side door of the Peters' residence. Caryn and Mary Ann ran off together and took cover behind the Ellsberg's place (yes, THE Ellsbergs of Watergate fame; neighbors across the street I never knew until they made headline news).

Moments later, a police car drove slowly down the street, shining a big flashlight up and around each house it passed, first on one side of the street, then the other. Lucky for John they were coming east down the street instead of west or the probing light would have nailed him.

Whenever this group gathered together for their nightly forays in the neighborhood, it was understood that if a police car was spotted, they ran. It was called, "Hassling the Cops". And it was Grand Fun!

Just one of the many pranks pulled by this rag-tag group of boys and girls who lived across the street from each other back in those halcyon days of teen, pre-teen, youth, circa 1976. Their mothers were 'cuppa coffee' neighbors who exchanged recipes, neighborhood gossip, and parenting tips along with their coffee. One had six kids, one had four. There was always plenty to talk about.

Getting together for dinner 20 years later to reminisce about those times, which in retrospect seem so innocent, made for a delightful evening.

* * * * *

Me and my neighbor, Joyce.

She had six kids, all adopted. The two oldest were twin girls. They began babysitting for me when they were about 14. Next came Pat, a year younger; then Robbie, a year younger than Pat; then Tom and then Mary Anne.

My four were Tom, the oldest; John, a year and a half younger; then Caryn, 18 months younger than John. Lisa, my youngest, was mostly out of the loop as far as the group shenanigans of 1979 were concerned. She was too little. Except she did have the reputation as the neighborhood delinquent. At the grand old age of two yet. I'll explain that later.

One of the funniest things I remember occurred when Julie, one of the twins, was babysitting. Jerry and I had gone out to eat and to a movie. Julie and Joyce took turns sitting for us; they were about sixteen at the time. This night it was Julie. She love to knit and crochet and often brought her projects with her for when the kids had gone to bed.

Whenever we returned from our evenings out, we would always ask the girls, regardless of which one had showed up that evening to babysit, "How did it go? Did you have any trouble?" "No, no; the kids were great. No trouble at all." That was all we ever heard.

Years later we learned their mother, Joyce, had told them when they first started babysitting, "if you're old enough to babysit, you're old enough to handle the problems." So, of course, we never learned of any problems. At the time

But then, my kids, now grown, began to "confess" to all sorts of activities and escapades that ended up being considerably different from what I thought at the time.

The babysitting incident being one of funniest and least delinquent in nature.

It happened like this.

One night Julie brought her yarn and sat happily crocheting and watching TV after she got the kids to bed. I don't know how long it was before she realized something had happened. Quiet as mice, two boys had slipped downstairs and pulled off large amounts of yarn from the ball of yarn so Julie would have plenty of yarn at her disposal and not realize what else was going on. Then they started "weaving" the remaining yarn up the stairs, into the bedrooms, into the bathroom, down the stairs, into the hall, into the bathroom, et cetera et cetera.

I wish I could have been there when Julie finally reached the end of her available yarn and felt a tug at the other end!

When we got home that night, we asked our usual, "how we're the kids?" "Oh, fine. Just fine," she said. Right. I hope at least she made **them** unwind it.

We have all laughed about this many times in the years since.

Too bad all their shenanigans weren't so innocent.

*****

Like the time I had to go to the police station to pick up my eldest, Tom, who was about 15 at the time. He sat there and I sat there and we listened to the officer explain that Tom and his buddy had been caught throwing lighted matches in the trash that had been set out by all the neighbors for pick up early the next morning.

"Oh, no; you're mistaken. Tom didn't do it. He told me he didn't. And he wouldn't lie to me. He's such a good kid, really. You've just made a terrible mistake." And then I started to cry. I was indignant and hurt that he would accuse MY son. The officer must have thought I was quite a Dip! And had all he could do to keep his patience with me. It wasn't until I got back home, talked with Tom some more, talked with Jerry, and finally got it through my head that Tom, did, of course, do it.

* * * * *

One of the favorite things the boys did was sneak out of their rooms after everyone had gone to bed. The grade school was just six blocks away and it had an Olympic-size swimming pool outside on the school property. My children had taken lessons and swam there every summer. Our community had an excellent school system and recreation program, which was one reason we had moved there back in 1963.

In the summer, they would sneak out only in their underwear (why? I still don't know.) and jog over to the swimming pool for a late night swim. Of course, if they encountered a police car patrolling the neighborhood, they played their usual game and took off running.

This particular night, however, Jerry and I had gone out and come home a little earlier than planned. Jerry stuck his head in John's bedroom as a matter of course as fathers and mothers often do to check on their sleeping "angels".

Lo and behold, there is no "angel". And a window is ajar!

That "angel" had quite a surprise waiting for him a few minutes later when, after an hour or two of frolicking in the pool, he stuck his wet little butt through the window and found his father sitting waiting on his bed!

* * * * *

Then there was the time when Caryn and Lisa, about nine and six-and-a-half or seven, were discovered smoking upstairs in our alcove by their father (a smoker).

Our house had two bedrooms and a bath downstairs and two bedrooms and a bath upstairs. One upstairs bedroom had a walk-in closet with a short door that led to an alcove off the closet. You could stand upright in the middle and we often talked about finishing it up as another bedroom with built-in beds on either of the sloped sides. But we never did.

It was a great play house for the kids, however. (How did Jerry discover them up there, anyway???)

So Jerry sat there with them and made them each smoke a cigarette – all the way down – to the stub – in his presence. Caryn cried and choked and spit and had a terrible time. "I'll never, ever do this again, dad. I promise."

Then it was the six-year-old's turn; Lisa. She didn't choke. She didn't spit. She didn't cry. Not once. She smoked that cigarette all the way down as though she had done it all her life. That was Lisa. Tough. On the outside. She would never let you see her hurt or cry.

Except sometimes me, she let.

(Thank you, darlin' Pie.)

* * * * *

There was one other time the police brought Tom and John home. I think I was at work. So they had to deal with Jerry and I heard about it later.

The police had discovered them in the park and accused them of smoking marijuana. The story I heard was the police found the marijuana stubs on the ground near them.

Same thing from me, of course. "Well, I don't think they did it. Did you see them do it? If we didn't see them do it, then how can we accuse them?"

This from me because with four kids running around getting into each other's stuff all the time I had always told them not to accuse each other of doing or taking something unless they saw the person do it. So when it came to discipline, I tried to follow the same rules I asked of them. I tried to practice not blaming them for something unless I had the facts.

In retrospect, I have learned this marked me as "a pushover, mom."

But that's okay. Believing in and expecting the best from your kids – that's what Moms do.

* * * * *

When I was a child I had a series of books (How and Why Library) my mom read to me. One was a book of poems and "moral" stories. I loved it. One poem was entitled, "Mr. Nobody". Mr. Nobody was the one who did all the bad stuff, of course.

So when things would happen in our house, we often joked that Mr. Nobody did it. For instance, the spaghetti string splotched up on the dining room ceiling? Mr. Nobody. And the week's worth of treats suddenly gone missing? Mr. Nobody.

* * * * *

Speaking of those treats . . .

Dinnertime was a specific regular event in our home in those family years. We all sat down together at the table and everyone talked about his day. It was just the regular thing we did every night.

With four kids and limited funds for groceries, I would buy juice and koolaid and treats, enough for a week at a time, and then I would portion them out on a daily basis. This usually worked pretty good though once in awhile someone might sneak an extra.

One night in particular, we had finished eating and the kids wanted a treat for desert. But we couldn't find the treats! I had just bought a week's worth so it got to be quite a serious issue and Jerry was really upset. He'd asked each of the kids, "who took the treats?", but no one would admit to taking any. The thing that bothered him was thinking one or all of them were lying.

Finally he sent them all to Tom's room with the instruction, "you guys go in there and get to the bottom of this. Someone took them. Don't come back out till you get a confession."

It seemed they were in there forever! Finally, John came out and ran out to the garage. At that time we would take the garbage out daily, set it in the garage, and then one of the kids had the task of taking it to the street for pick-up on the day the trash people came.

John had decided he would go through each bag of garbage, just in case. They had racked their brains trying to figure out what had happened. For once, they were not guilty as charged.

Sure enough, the treats were in the garage! They had been in a big black plastic bag sitting in the kitchen and whoever took out the trash accidentally included that bag with the trash!

* * * * *

Our front door opened into a vestibule with a closet on one side, another door with a stairway going upstairs on the other side, and an open entry straight ahead into the living room. The two girls shared one bedroom upstairs and Jerry and I had the other. The boys each had a bedroom downstairs.

One night Jerry and I had been out for the evening and I headed upstairs for bed. When I opened the door to the stairway, a "thing" came sliding down the hand rail at me. I screamed and ducked! It was a large white T-shirt made to look something like a ghost and it was attached to a hangar and some string in a way that when I opened the door it came sliding down the bannister!

Or the time I came racing into the house about 9:30 p.m., home from my part-time evening sales job at Sears, running into the bathroom having to pee . . . really bad . . . didn't even take time to turn on the bathroom light and – why is the lid down??? – quickly pushing up the lid so I can sit down . . . only to find a rubber snake taped to the seat!

After my blood-curdling screams subsided . . . I believe I heard smothered laughter coming from the boys' room down the hall.

* * * * *

And then there was the time Tom pitched a third of our driveway out into the street. Well, actually, he didn't INTEND to. It just "happened" the way things "happen" when kids are being kids.

He was about 14 at the time. Old enough to want to drive, not old enough to do so. Except. My reward to him for helping me get the carful of groceries into the kitchen every week was to let him pull the car up into the drive. I would park it just off the street and into our driveway, we would lug the groceries in, and then he would move the car up on the driveway as far as it would go. We didn't have a garage at the time so the driveway was only about 20 feet long.

This particular time, we had gotten home about 20 minutes before Jerry was expected, which was 5:30 p.m. Jerry was usually prompt.

Once I got inside with the groceries I was oblivious to what was taking place in the driveway. Years later I learned it was his practice to drive the car back and forth, back and forth as many times as he thought he could get away with. This time, however, after he drove it back (toward the street), he decided to "nail it" going forward.

* * * * *

I have to digress for a moment and interject this bit of information. "Years later" was when we were in Michigan for a few days and planned a dinner get-together with my neighbor Joyce and a couple of her kids and she told us she just happened to be watching this entire incident from her front window.

* * * * *

When Tom "nailed" it, large junks of asphalt from the driveway went exploding off the driveway into the street! The asphalt had been down for many years and was full of cracks. The stress from the weight of the spinning tires of a 2-1/2 ton station wagon was too much.

Inside, I was blissfully unaware of the drama being played outside on the driveway but Joyce saw it all.

Tom knew his dad would be home any minute so he scrambled about getting all the pieces of asphalt out of the street and back into some semblance of order in the driveway. Somehow he managed to accomplish this before his dad arrived!

At our recent dinner, Joyce told us she just stood there at her window laughing and thinking, "Oh, Boy, Sarah's in for it now."

* * * * *

When John was two, he loved to play hide and seek. Except he would stand in front of you with his hands over his eyes and say, "go find me, mom, go find me." I guess he thought since he couldn't see me, I couldn't see him.

* * * * *

Patrick. He was Joyce's oldest boy. Next in age to the twins. Tow-headed and friendly and lovable as a pup. All these kids were good kids. They all had jobs and responsibilities of one sort or another the whole time they were growing up. Patrick, especially, always seemed to look out for the younger kids.

One of the neighbors down the street had an in-ground pool in their backyard and they invited the neighborhood children over for a pool party one summer afternoon. They were an older couple, had no children at home, but they loved kids still. Moms were invited. I think they even served snacks.

So the moms were standing around visiting and the kids were splashing and jumping and playing in the pool. For some reason Patrick was not in the pool. Probably he came over to ask his mom something. All of a sudden he yelled and dove into the middle of the pool and grabbed his little sister. She must have been about 6 or 7 at the time. They all could swim, at least a little bit, but I guess she got in over her head and panicked and started to gasp and choke. And in jumped Patrick to the rescue!

At our dinner Joyce told us that, after we moved away and as the kids got older, she and Mickey started taking a week's vacation in Las Vegas every year. One year when they got home and walked into their front vestibule, she sniffed and sniffed and finally yelled out to the gang of kids hurriedly assembling in their living room, "Okay, who had the party, what did you do, and why was it necessary to paint the walls?"

Or the time 17-year-old Rob borrowed the family car – Joyce and Mickey were on their yearly Vegas hiatus – and tore up the engine. Somehow he knew somebody who knew somebody and he got it replaced before they returned. It just cost him his next three months' salary, however. Doled out a week at a time.

Some lessons sure are expensive!

Which, in turn, led to . . .

– The Story of Pie –
Lisa Danielle. My youngest of four.

At first she was Dani. From the time she was born till she started school. Because Jerry and I thought Dani was a delightful nickname for Danielle. We liked the idea of having a little girl who was kind of a tomboy so that was another reason we liked it. Because she was; tomboyish. Independent too. Jerry called her his little terror and said she bossed him and everyone else around.

She became Lisa when she started school because the teachers called her by her first name and we gradually got into the habit also.

Being the youngest, she always wanted to do whatever the older ones were doing. Often, too often as far as Caryn was concerned, I made her take Lisa along when she played with her neighbor friend, Mary Ann McGowan. They got even, of course, by teasing her and putting her up to stunts (like the Bea Olmstead affair recounted in the next section). And they made up their own nickname -- Lisa, Piece-A-Possum- Pooh. Except when they said it around the family, they changed it to Lisa Pizza Pie. Then the boys picked up on that and for a variation called her Izza Pizza Pie. When she was little, this made her mad and she would cry from their teasing.

Eventually, her brothers and sister outgrew their need to tease her this way and she became Pie or The Pie and, most recently, Her Pieness. It had, finally, become our affectionate nickname for her and eventually she understood and accepted it that way too. To this day. She recently moved to Franklin (where the rest of us now reside) and the last message I got from her she signed as, "The Tennessee Pie."

I love it!

But before that she was . . .

— The Delinquent of Huntington Woods —

Too frequently, I suppose, it fell upon Caryn to watch and/or play with her little sister. Much to her chagrin. But she and Mary Ann devised ways of getting even. As previously referenced in the Lisa, Piece-A Possum Pooh story.

This is a story about the time they got her to go over to Bea Olmstead's house, knock on the door, and say, "I Hate You."

Bea Olmstead lived directly across the street from us. She was a retired school administrator. She and her husband had been teachers early in their careers. Mr. Olmstead had passed away many years ago. Bea still perceived herself to be an important part of her community. She had teas and entertained often. Always had Open House at Christmas and other holidays.

One Sunday afternoon when she was having company, she came over and asked our kids to move their toys out of our front yard and lawn because she thought it looked unsightly for her company. (!) (?) When the kids told their dad, he promptly had them drag every toy they owned (as well as those from the neighbors) out to our front yard!

This particular incident occurred when Caryn and Mary Ann told Lisa, who was just past two, to go over to Mrs. Olmstead, who was working in her yard, and say, "I Hate You."

Naturally Lisa did it. Twice! Because the first time, Mrs. Olmstead ignored her. So they sent her back. The second time Bea grabbed her up, shook her, and yelled at her.

Mickey McGowan, Mary Ann's father, just happened to be outside in his yard and saw the incident. He lived two houses down from Bea. Although he surely couldn't have heard what Bea said to Lisa, he saw her grab her and shake her and yell something. He was probably amazed that an adult would take offense at something a baby would say. He came over and told Bea to stop. They exchanged some heated words. Later Mickey came over and told Jerry what had happened.

Jerry waited until he saw Bea leave her house. I believe he confronted her in the middle of the street! I think he grabbed her arm and said, "Don't ever lay a hand on one of my children again!" Then this 70-year-old lady threatened to beat him up. Jerry, in turn, threatened to call the police.

Bea didn't speak to us for over a year. Then one day she came over shortly after Jerry got home from work. He went to the door. She had a box of candy in her hands and said, "I'm sorry. Let's be friends again." Jerry said, "No thanks. I prefer things just the way they are," and abruptly closed the door in her face!

The Huntington Woods Delinquent and Her Posse . . .

Summer 1972

2-Year Old On A Mission, Sent by Caryn & Mary Ann

"Go Tell Bea Olmstead, 'I Hate You'

Summer 1973

Huntington Woods Delinquent and Her Posse

Caryn, Mary Ann, Dani (Pie)

The "House Full of Kids"
10075 Vernon,
Huntington Woods, Michigan
Circa 1978

The Car, The Boy, The Driveway (*)

Accross the Street, 3 Houses Down Standing in Her Yard is my Neighboor, Joyce, watching the drama unfold the night Tom pitched several sections of asphalt into the street "gunning the gas" up and down the driveway and then frantically attempting to get it all back in place before his father arrived home.

And Life Goes On . . .

To Be Continued . . .

Sarah's Journey, Through the Years

Wherein Sarah Speaks Of

**Parents and Aging
And Nonsense and Heros
And Wars . . . and Dying . . . and Then . . .
Another Family Tragedy**

www.ingramcontent.com/pod-product-compliance
Lightning Source LLC
Chambersburg PA
CBHW032003220426
43664CB00005B/127